# TEACHING KINDERGARTEN CHILDREN

By
LOIS HORTON YOUNG

Philadelphia
**THE JUDSON PRESS**

Chicago                                                           Los Angeles

© The Judson Press 1959

All rights in this book are reserved. No part of the book may be reproduced in any manner without permission in writing from the publisher, except in the case of brief quotations included in a review of the book in a magazine or newspaper.

Cover Design: Sylvia Polis

This book has been prepared to give guidance on teaching kindergarten children. Both teachers and parents will find much practical help. In addition it is recommended as a textbook for one of the First Series courses of the New Standard Leadership Curriculum. Full information regarding these courses will be found in *Leadership Education Handbook* which may be ordered from The Judson Press.

Printed in U.S.A.

# CONTENTS

|  | PAGE |
|---|---|
| "Why" | 5 |

CHAPTER

| 1. Knowing the Children | 13 |
|---|---|
| 2. Living with Children at Church | 31 |
| 3. Knowing and Using Curriculum Materials | 46 |
| 4. Helping Children to Learn | 57 |
| 5. Obtaining a Good Group Response | 85 |
| 6. Working on a Team | 99 |
| Bibliography | 111 |

# "WHY"

"Why does the sun go down every night?" asks Jan. "Why does a bulldozer make that noise?" "Why can't I stay up till ten o'clock?" "Why does Aunt Midge talk all the time?" Why, why, why? The four- or five-year-old asks many, many questions — any kind of question, but especially "why" questions. One of the jobs of the grownups who live with him is to help him to find answers that will be satisfying to him.

To adequately answer children's questions, we must first find the answers to our own. But we must also maintain a seeking mind which looks for reasons and keeps growing.

Let us pause on the threshold of this adventure in learning and ask ourselves two "why" questions. First: Why am I reading this book? Take a pencil and write your answer before you read another word. . . .

Are you reading it because you want to be a good kindergarten teacher, or a better one? Do you want to understand children of this fascinating age and know how to bring them to know the God you love? Or perhaps you are looking for a field of Christian service and you feel your interest drawing you toward teaching kindergarten, so you wish to explore its possibilities. You may be seeking to discover specific ways of working effectively in the kindergarten room. Whether you are a parent, an active teacher, or a potential teacher, if any of these are your reasons, this book is for YOU!

And now, on to the next "why" question. Why do we want children to come to the church kindergarten? Reasons in the minds of parents, if we could only read them, would vary widely. They would range all the way from accepting the convenience of a free Sunday morning baby-sitting service (it sounds unbelievable but it's actual and factual), to the highest and best reasons which might be given by a teacher.

The goal for which we are working and which we must

always keep clearly in mind is like a prism with many facets. As light falls upon a prism and is changed into specific colors, so each activity we introduce into the experience of kindergarten children in the church must bring about some change in their ideas, feelings, and actions. The child, through an activity, should experience growth in some of the ways described in the following objectives for the Christian education of kindergarten children. Only when this is true of an activity have we the right to include it in the kindergarten program of the Sunday church school.

## THE CHILD AND GOD

God has planned that the child should grow in body, mind, and spirit. The child's spiritual growth depends on his *growing relationship with God* expressed through love for God and confidence and faith in him. This is basic to an abundant Christian life. By the time a child is four years old, if he has been with Christian parents and teachers he should have begun *to sense the greatness and wonder and love of God,* and to associate God with all that is good in his own life. If a child has not had Christian guidance during these early years, then we will have to lay the foundations when he becomes of kindergarten age.

Through the kindergarten years we will seek to provide experiences at home and at church which will encourage the child's loving response to God and help him *to know more about God.* As he enjoys the world about him we will lead him *to think* more directly *of God as the Creator of this wonderful world* and to feel a sense of satisfaction in belonging to it. We will help him *to discover that God not only loves him but also desires his love.* God's love includes all people and he calls upon us to love one another.

Through all his experiences with the world of nature and of persons we will try to lead the kindergarten child *to feel a sense of fellowship with God* who is still actively at work in his world. We will help him *to feel a love for God* that finds expression in joyous worship and in efforts to work with him as a little child may. We will lead the child *to know that he can talk with God* naturally about his interests, for God wants to hear the things that make the child glad and God is ready to forgive and help him when things go wrong, or when he fails to do what is right and good.

Above all, we who are parents and teachers will try to grow in our own experience of God and to live according to his purposes, for it is through living with growing Christian persons that the kindergarten child best comes to know God. Our faith can help him begin *to find in God security* in the midst of the fears that beset even young children today.

## THE CHILD AND JESUS

Our major responsibility and our joyous privilege as teachers and parents is to guide the child toward an eventual acceptance of Jesus Christ as Savior, presenting to him as he grows older the matchless life of Jesus and sharing with him our own faith. With the nursery child we laid firm foundations for the kind of growing love for and knowledge of Jesus that will make it possible in later years for the Holy Spirit to lead the child to accept Christ as his Savior. Before he is four, *the child should know about Jesus, whom God sent as a baby and think of him as a friend whom he knows and loves.*

During the kindergarten years it is our responsibility to build on this foundation so that the child *feels a growing love for Jesus.* We will help him *to form increasingly clear ideas of Jesus as one who was a kind and loving friend and from whom we learn what God is like.* Because we want him to grow steadily toward the point where he will accept Jesus Christ as Savior with real understanding, we will share with him in these years stories of Jesus' life on earth. We will avoid confusing Jesus, the Son of God, with God the Father; and we will address our prayers to God as Jesus taught us to do. Since little children are very literal-minded we will avoid abstract and symbolic terms and those ideas that are beyond their experience and comprehension.

We will help the kindergarten child *to grow in his understanding of the way of life that Jesus showed to men* by directing his thought to what Jesus said and did. By bringing him into contact with persons who are Christlike and guiding him to use opportunities in his home, church, and neighborhood for putting into practice Jesus' way of living, we will help him *to develop a fuller appreciation of what the Christian way means.*

## THE CHILD AND THE BIBLE

We believe that God speaks to us through the Bible and therefore we want the Bible to have a vital place in the life of every child. For this reason we introduced the nursery child to the Bible with great care through conversation about it and simple stories and verses from it that he could make his own. By the time a child is four years old he should *recognize the Bible as the special book* in which we read about God and Jesus, a book which is valued and loved by his parents and teachers.

Through the kindergarten years it is our privilege *to increase the child's appreciation of the Bible* in many ways. We will help him *to find satisfaction in knowing and using simple verses* to express his own joy and confidence, and to begin to use Bible truths in his own everyday living. Because his needs and understanding are broadening we will find it possible *to use repeatedly with the child more stories and verses* than he was able to understand before he was four. By means of dramatic play, music, and pictures we will *deepen the child's enjoyment and appreciation of the Bible.* We will keep an attractive copy of the Bible in the kindergarten room and refer to it frequently.

As parents and teachers we will show that we enjoy the Bible, use it and value it as the Word of God, for our attitude of appreciation will increase the child's sense of its importance.

## THE CHILD AND THE CHURCH

Loyalty to his church through the years, and joy and satisfaction in his church life are our goals for every child. Before a child is four he should come *to think of his church as a special place where he feels at home, where families and good friends enjoy being together to worship and work and learn more about God and Jesus.*

During the kindergarten years we will help the child *to learn more about his church and to become better acquainted with the church family — the minister, his teachers, and other adult and child friends.* We will lead him *to love his church and to feel himself a loved and respected member* of the church family, *doing his part* as he comes there to work, play, and worship with friends, and share with others through gifts and service. We will help him to begin *to think about boys and girls who enjoy going to their churches in our land and other lands,* thus laying a foundation for his realization that the fellowship of Christians is a great world family. Above all, we will set him an example of loyalty and glad participation in the church's life and program, for our attitude toward the church as parents and teachers will do more than anything else to help the child reach the goal of a true appreciation of the church.

## THE CHILD'S PERSONAL GROWTH

A wholesome Christian character essential to a full and abundant life is a part of God's will for every person. The foundations for such a character are laid in the very earliest years. While the child was of nursery age he should have begun *to discover that he is a person of worth and ability who can do things for himself.* He should have begun *to realize that what he does affects others;* that there are *satisfactions in sharing;* and that in both the joy of succeeding and the disappointment of failing *he can turn to God naturally,* expressing thanks and asking help day by day.

In the kindergarten years we will help the child to grow further in all of these ways, giving him many opportunities both at home and at church *to practice Christian living day by day* and to direct his actions by the Bible truths he is learning.

Through careful guidance in everyday experiences we will help him *to grow in his ability to work and play happily alone and with others.* We will encourage him *to share attention and materials with others,* and to begin to be willing to give up his own way. We will also encourage him *to try to do what his parents and teachers depend on him to do,* and to acknowledge his mistakes and mishaps. As we do this we will be helping the child *to develop self-control* and some ability to assume responsibility and self-direction for his conduct. This is the beginning of self-discipline.

In all of these everyday experiences and in special experiences of disappointment, suffering and wrongdoing we will help the child through conversation and prayer *to rely on God's concern for him as a person* and *to find satisfaction in talking with God about his own problems and interests.*

## THE CHILD AND OTHERS

God's love reaches out toward all people and he expects us to love our neighbor as ourselves. The nursery child made only a small beginning in recognizing this truth, for only gradually could he become aware of the needs and rights of others. We introduced him to a few people outside his home and nursery group and encouraged him *to be friendly* toward them while trying to surround him at home and at church with persons who in their living expressed true Christian concern for others.

The kindergarten child has widening contacts beyond his home and often is forming attitudes toward people of other races and lands which affect his relationship with others. We will help the child both in his everyday contacts and in special experiences provided for him to begin *to understand that God loves all people and that others have equal rights with him.*

Since the kindergarten child is still self-centered we ought not to expect much maturity in putting others first. We will guide him *to make definite progress,* however, *in becoming a helpful, co-operating member of the group as he learns to share, take turns, and consider the rights of others.* We will encourage him *to respond in friendly ways to others,* to show sympathy for those who are ill or lonely and to find joy in performing simple services for them. We will help him to begin *to appreciate the contributions others make to his own well-being and happiness,* and to grow in his understanding that God's plan includes all people.

We will help him to begin to see that the church is one way we work together to help others. We will give him opportunities to begin *to feel himself a part of the church's missionary outreach through sharing* in service projects and giving his money with some understanding of how it is used.

We will help him *to learn something about people who live*

*in other parts of the world and to begin to think with appreciation and interest of these other members of the world family* who work and play and learn in ways similar to his own. As we develop in him this beginning interest in others we will be laying foundations for his growing concern to share the story of Jesus with all people who do not know him.

## HOW?

This book is concerned with helping you to discover ways of setting about to accomplish the objectives stated above. It will not "give you all the answers," but it will certainly challenge your thinking and guide your doing as you prepare for what we think is one of life's most exciting adventures — teaching kindergarten children!

12

CHAPTER 1

# KNOWING THE CHILDREN

Let's look in on a Kindergarten Department on Sunday morning. The children are busy with early activities, for the session is just under way. We can immediately feel a special quality in the atmosphere of this room. It comes not only from the color and lightness and brightness and interest of the room itself, but it comes from the people in it. We watch Mrs. Dixon moving among the group and somehow gain the feeling that she has set the tone of the room, for wherever she goes she has an effect on the atmosphere. Bruce has just joined Ken in the block corner. Ken's manner suggests that the newcomer is scarcely welcome! Quietly Mrs. Dixon becomes a part of the situation, and though we cannot hear what she says, we see Ken's attitude changing; he is accepting Bruce as a partner in his project.

Another teacher sits down beside a child who is drawing a picture and talks with her about her work. As the teacher comments, Pat talks about her picture and smiles, then works with even greater enjoyment. Bill is having trouble with his puzzle, and there is a teacher, not to do it for him, but to show him how turning all the pieces right side up will help, and how turning one piece around slowly will make it fit. The children accept help and respond in a wholesome, happy fashion to the teacher's presence. We know immediately that here is a teacher who loves each child, who knows him, who feels with him, who understands him, who has something vital to share. And we know that this makes for good teaching and ready learning in that kindergarten room!

## LOVING THEM

As in Mrs. Dixon's room, so in every kindergarten room, the teachers set the tone for relationships within the room. The teacher's relationship with each child as a person is basic and is itself based on his own personal relationship with God. As God's love fills the life of the teacher, that teacher has an overflow of love to share with the children. Like God himself, who sees more than outward appearance, this teacher sees beyond the blond curls and brown pigtails, beyond the ruffly dresses and patched shirts, beyond the healthy young bodies and the thin faltering ones, beyond the clear blue eyes and the puzzled brown ones peering through thick lenses. This teacher sees the essential worth of each child; seeks to see the world through the child's eyes; to feel with him; to know his ideas, his problems, his wonder. He finds in the child an essential self to love, to cherish, to cultivate. The overaggressive child, the withdrawn one, and the restless can't-sit-a-minute one are as attractive to him as the child who has "perfect behavior." The cross-eyed child, the oversized one, and the slow-learning one are as lovable to this teacher as the adorable darling that everyone "ohs" and "ahs" about — perhaps more so, because of their special need for love and acceptance.

Children know this teacher's genuineness and instinctively trust him. They respond to the teacher's interest and love with a love and loyalty of their own. As the Sundays come and go, there is built up between child and teacher a relationship that makes for maximum learning, because the child is *ready* to learn and the teacher's understanding guides him in presenting a learning experience.

This teacher's love is not made up of gushing "Isn't he precious?" and "She is *so* cute!" remarks. It is made up of honest evaluation which might lead him to say, "I am proud of you; you are trying so hard!" or, "That was a very friendly thing to do, Jim!"

The teacher who really loves the kindergarten child possesses an outgiving love. Such a teacher never will be satisfied until he has shared his Christian faith with each child in everyday terms which the child can easily understand and, in a measure, absorb. This teacher never will be satisfied until he finds the *why* of each child's behavior. He always is looking for the underlying reason for what the child says and does; always trying to discover the thoughts and feelings behind actions. This helps the teacher to know the stage of growth of each child so he can effectively reach the child where he is and guide him in growing toward Christian maturity.

## LISTENING TO THEM

We all accept the fact that children learn from what grownups say, but many of us have not discovered that grownups may learn much from what children say. We gain valuable insights into what a child thinks and feels as we listen to the things he says — to us, to other grownups, to his friends, and, sometimes, to himself. The child's questions, comments, and conversation reveal his ideas and his attitudes and, for the careful observer, throw light on his motives, his problems, his growth.

Facial expressions, actions and reactions speak also. They speak less plainly than words, and yet so very clearly sometimes that a sensitive teacher or parent can interpret the meaning even though no words are spoken. It is by listening to what behavior says that the grownup becomes aware of the needs of a child; needs which he often is unable to put into words, and of which he himself is unconscious. Let us look at some behavior which has been observed in kindergarten groups and see what inner needs of the child this behavior reveals.

Carolyn says hardly a word during the entire session. She chooses activities she can do alone, and makes no social approaches to other children. The teacher tries to make a place for her in the group by calling attention to her good crayon picture, and by suggesting that Anne "be Carolyn's special friend" and sit near her or work with her throughout the session. Carolyn accepts the interest but makes little outward response. To the teacher Carolyn's behavior may be saying, "I need security. I am not sure other people are completely to be trusted. I am not sure of myself. I need friends, but I don't know how to make friends. Please help me."

Jim, on the other hand, talks constantly. He always wants

to be first. He tells the other children what to do. He insists on having a turn. He likes to say, "See what I can do." And, if the teacher commends another child, *he* always asks for commendation too. Jim's behavior may be saying, "I need to be important. I need recognition. I need approval. I need to know that I matter." The teacher hears what his behavior says, and gives him recognition and reassurance whenever possible. Occasionally it may be before the group, but often it is done quietly, to him alone.

Jay seems to gain satisfaction from doing whatever he "isn't supposed to do." When the group is listening to a story, he makes noises with his feet, watching for the teacher's reaction. When the teacher asks him to carry his chair carefully, he picks it up over his head. When told that it is time to put away the blocks, he kicks them over and dawdles at putting them away. To the suggestion that he hang up his coat, he gives an outright "No!" Jay's behavior might be saying many things, but knowing his background, the teacher guesses he is trying to say, "I need limits. I find the world pretty unpredictable. Sometimes adults react one way to what I do, sometimes the other. I'm trying to find some consistent pattern. Please show me where the fences are. What may I do, and what may I not do?"

Pat always sits as close to the teacher as possible, eager to show the things he does. He comes often during the session to ask or tell the teacher something. If the teacher puts his arm around him, he snuggles close. Pat may be saying by his behavior, "I need love. I need attention. I don't get quite enough to satisfy my deepest needs in other places. Please let me know that *you* love me."

Paul never seems to want help. He works at his problems independently whether he is struggling with a zipper or working a puzzle. He resents interference or assistance from another child or a grownup. Linda, on the other hand, is always saying, "I can't" and "I don't know how." She asks help with every little thing. Both of these children could be saying by their behavior, "Please understand me. I need understanding!" Paul's actions might say, "I want to have a chance to try things, to learn to be independent, to grow!" while Linda's might say, "Everyone has always done things for me. I don't trust myself to do it right, and besides, I've never learned that there are things I have to do. It takes much less effort to have somebody do them for me!" And the teacher, hearing what behavior says, understands!

## FEELING WITH THEM

Being able to think children's thoughts is important for the kindergarten teacher, but no less important is being able to feel what they feel. Thoughts are colored by feelings, and feelings frequently determine our readiness to learn and are major factors in determining our growth in every area — physical, mental, social, and spiritual. The importance of emotions has been emphasized in many studies in recent years, for emotions frequently overrule thoughts in our behavior, and play a major part in determining our adjustment to other people and to the world around us. To be a good kindergarten teacher it is necessary to feel what kindergarten children feel. This applies in all three areas to which we sometimes refer in terms of feeling — the child's physical response to conditions in the room, his response to sensory stimuli, and his inner emotional response to a situation.

**Feelings about his kindergarten room.** The child's attitude toward the church, as well as his feelings about what he learns there, may be conditioned by his feeling-response to the many specific aspects of the learning situation in his kindergarten room. If his feeling-response to his experiences in the kindergarten room is a happy one, the effect on his Christian growth will be different from the effect achieved when he reacts uncomfortably to those experiences.

Can you understand the child's feelings in the following situations? How does it feel to:

    sit on a chair when your feet won't touch the floor?

    try to see a picture the teacher is holding up in front of a window?

    have to work at a table that is as high as your shoulders?

    wait for somebody to get materials out and have nothing to do?

    be alone in a strange place with strange people?

    have to sit and sit and listen to someone when you aren't interested?

have to stop doing something you're enjoying, right in the middle of it?

be asked to look at a picture four or five feet above your head?

have to listen to someone going on and on in the same tone of voice and using words you don't understand?

be in a room that's hot and stuffy; or a room that's cold and damp?

be hurried off to be with a lot of people when you haven't had enough sleep?

spend time in a drab, poorly lighted, uninteresting room?

Put yourself in the child's place in each of the above situations and you will see that there is definitely a feeling connected with each situation, a feeling that will determine learning, especially if two or more of these are combined.

The good kindergarten teacher is alert to the physical conditions in the room at all times and insists that they be the kind of conditions which will give the children a happy, comfortable feeling about the place the church has provided for them.

**Feelings aroused through sensory stimuli.** Grownups tend to think of learning mainly as something which comes in through the eyes and the ears. A kindergarten teacher must be able to appreciate the importance of the other senses to the four- and five-year-old. The teacher must feel *with* children, and know that unless they touch and taste and smell, their yen for learning is not satisfied. They *have* to touch things.

A teacher, showing another teacher a superior quality of finger paint paper said, "Just *feel* this!" The four-year-olds within earshot crowded around clambering, "Let me feel it!" So the paper was laid on the table and each had a chance to touch it and tell what it felt like. The answers showed their sensitivity to finger feelings as they said with delight, "A soapy bathtub!" "Ice cubes," "Waxy floor," "Turtle water."

It is at this point that we must be alert to offer opportunities for children to enjoy sensations of color, of sound, of softness and sharpness, of sweetness and fragrance, and to help them associate the wonder of these with God. So we have "wonder tables," we go for walks, we have flowers in the room, we let children touch and sometimes taste things. We feel *with* them and know their eagerness to share an experience to the full; to find out.

Knowing that feelings of wonder are close to worship we seize such lovely shining moments and hold them in a wisp of silence, then put the feeling into simple words and often, a brief prayer of thanks and praise.

Being able to feel with children, you, the kindergarten teacher (man or woman), can use the voice more effectively and know that a low, well-modulated voice has the power to impart feelings of strength and confidence, while a high-pitched or rapid voice stirs feelings of irritability or overstimulation. When you tell a story, share in a conversation or pray, vary the pitch, tempo and volume of your voice to convey feeling. Train your voice to respond to your own feeling and to create a similar feeling in the child. Speak in vibrant tones of joy, "Isn't it wonderful?" or genuine tones of sympathy, "I'm really sorry." Pray in a tone which makes the presence of God a reality, so that love and reverence are felt, without sanctimoniousness. Reflect the idea and mood of the moment in a story through an expressive voice. Children will listen and respond!

**Feelings are contagious.** The kindergarten teacher must be aware of children's inner emotional responses. The teacher can feel *with* the children and, in doing so, know that they will respond. They will pick up the emotional tone the teacher sets. Therefore, set a tone of steadiness, not irritability; deliberateness, not haste; matter-of-factness, not disturbed unevenness; assumption of co-operation, not apprehensiveness. Children will respond. (For example, have you ever known one *not* to respond when his hovering mama proclaimed, "I'm *sure* he's going to cry. He will never stay anywhere without me!" Naturally, Peter puckers into a ready-to-howl frown if mother starts to leave!)

Understanding children's feelings, the teacher works to strengthen the positive ones. One does not do this by using the poor, overworked, and ineffective generalities, "Be kind," and "Be good." It is done by giving feelings concrete guidance into action: "Ann, you will make Billy happy by sharing the truck with him" or, "These socks we are packing will make some children's toes cozy and warm." This requires the teacher to be deliberate in his thinking and speech.

Help children to understand their own feelings: "We are having a happy time because we are working together in a friendly way." Or, "It is really loving somebody when you help him."

But strengthening the positive feelings is only half the story. One must work to rechannel negative feelings, and always without condemnation. You might say, "I understand, George. We all feel angry sometimes. The important thing is to get rid of your bad feelings in a good way," and suggest that he punch a lump of clay or jump hard. (This is a practical kindergarten method for teaching the biblical injunction, "Be angry but do not sin" Eph. 4:26.)

When you sense that a child is afraid, explain his fears to him without ridicule and help him to discover that God is a resource worthy of trust and available to even a four-year-old. This is not theology beyond his comprehension; he accepts it more readily than the grownup, trusting willingly and instinctively.

So in the whole realm of feelings, the teacher tries to know the child, to accept him as he is, and to let this capacity of *feeling with him* give direction to all relationships with the children.

## UNDERSTANDING WHAT THEY ARE LIKE

What is the characteristic behavior of the four-to-six-year old? How may we expect the four-to-six-year-old to respond? What is the level of his development at this age? We can take the "guesswork" out of this question by referring to the collective experience of many parents and teachers who have worked with this age child, and to the data derived from numerous scientific studies. Such information is compiled in the charts on pages 22-25.

These studies are of basic importance to the prospective and the active kindergarten teacher. They reveal the growth pattern which may be expected and which will need to be taken into account in planning and carrying out a session with the children. With this pattern clearly in mind, the teacher will gain much from observing a kindergarten group.

Before studying this growth pattern, perhaps there should be a reminder that, although this is basic, the pattern has many variations. There are many individual differences, and when the basic pattern is very familiar to the teacher, there is the need to study the children in the group to see how each varies at some point from what might be expected. Some are mature in nearly every respect; some are immature in nearly every respect. Some show the mental traits of a six-year-old, are five chronologically, and three in their social development. Each child has special needs and capacities. Each may at times depart from his own pattern as growth slows in one area and speeds up in another. Each reacts to changing circumstances in his own life by some variation in behavior. Some circumstances which are particularly likely to cause variation are physical illness, absence of father on a trip, arrival of a new baby, emotional involvement of parents, mother going to work, economic pressures which children are permitted to feel, fears which disturb the child. Know the *cause* of behavior, and you will be more understanding.

## KNOWING CHILDREN IN RELATION TO THE CHRISTIAN EDUCATION OBJECTIVES FOR THIS AGE

As Christian adults, it is easy for us to visualize the eventual goal we have for each child. We want him to grow into Christian maturity, to grow up in every way into Christ (see Ephesians 4:15). But such growth is a long process; a process which calls for years of learning, of practice, of fellowship with God. Just how much of this growing should we expect to see accomplished at the kindergarten level? To determine this, it will be helpful to look at the objectives set forth in the beginning of this book. These objectives are defined in the light of two major considerations: (1) What ideas, feelings and actions do we hope to see developed in each individual when he arrives at maturity? (2) In the light of the characteristics of the four-to-six-year-old, what is possible for him to absorb at this age level which will lead him in the direction of our eventual goals? God's laws of growth are well

(Charts on pages 22-25, text continued on page 26)

# THE KINDERGARTEN CHILD

A kindergarten child is like this:

## I. Physically

1. He is constantly active and concerned with large-muscle activity. He is developing motor skills rapidly. Skill in use of body, legs, and arms develops before skill in the use of fingers and hands.

2. He becomes tired rapidly and shows it by restlessness, and the urge to sit or lie down, and sometimes by social difficulties.

3. He may do well in one motor skill and poorly in another. There is little relation between motor development and mental ability.

4. He is very susceptible to infectious diseases.

5. He learns more readily when physically comfortable.

## II. Mentally

1. Curiosity and eagerness to learn stimulate many questions and urge the child to ask, to see, to touch, taste, or smell. Experiences with the senses intensify learning.

2. His vocabulary develops rapidly and will range from about 1,500 to 2,000 words. He often confuses new words with similar-sounding, familiar ones and this results in confused ideas. A "cocoon" may become a "racoon" or a "diploma" a "plum" for example.

3. He enjoys sounds and sound-words. He experiments with nonsense words and appealing sound combinations.

4. His keen imagination makes imitation and impersonation very real. It sometimes makes him confuse the real with the imagined and leads him to accept fancy as fact. His limited information contributes to this confusion.

5. He wants to do things for himself and he learns most readily through *"doing."*

6. He learns rapidly, but greatly enjoys repetition of pleasant experiences.

# FROM FOUR TO SIX

## Therefore, leaders will do this:

### I. Physically

1. Alternate physically quiet times with active ones, and provide much opportunity for bodily motion. Provide more large muscle activities than small muscle activities. A sit-still-and-listen program is ineffective and unappealing to the child. Hand skill cannot be expected, but will make great strides between ages four and six.

2. Make adequate provision for rest. Plan this carefully to encourage relaxation.

3. Offer encouragement, be patient, and help at some points (in putting on wraps, or putting things away, for example). Suggest frequently that one child help another.

4. Be aware of ventilation, heating, draughts in the room. Insist that the room be clean, and hands washed before eating. Provide tissues for coughs and sneezes. Be familiar with signs of illness and be aware of the child who shows evidence of any of these. Avoid emphasizing regular attendance for that may lead sick children to expose others.

5. Provide adequate but not glaring lights and comfortable seating on floor or chairs. Good grouping and floor space will be real concerns.

### II. Mentally

1. Try to answer questions simply, satisfyingly, and yet in a way that stimulates the child's own thinking. Provide many sensory experiences which relate to the general or specific purposes of the session.

2. Choose words carefully in conversation, directions, and use of materials. Ask, "What is _____?" or "What does _____ mean?" if not sure the children know a word.

3. Provide rhythms and repetition of words in stories, conversation, and songs to increase attention. (Notice this in *My Bible Story Book,* for example.)

4. Do much teaching through various forms of dramatic play. Enter appreciatively into the child's imaginary experiences; help him to distinguish fact from fancy.

5. Give many opportunities for "doing" things which are within the child's capacity. Be alert for moments and situations where help is needed, but do not frustrate children by interfering with satisfying independent accomplishment.

6. Fill every session with much that is new and challenging, but make wise use of repetition, re-using enjoyed materials and procedures for better learning as well as the child's pleasure.

# THE KINDERGARTEN CHILD

## A kindergarten child is like this:

7. His interests are strongest in the colorful, the active, the familiar things, family and helpers, foods and animals, things that "go," outdoor wonders, workers, happy times and holidays. He has no grasp whatever of symbolism, and little sense of time or distance.

## III. Emotionally

1. Consistency and dependability in adults and surroundings contribute to his feeling of security. He likes to know where the limits are, and depends on adult support, approval, and supervision.

2. If he is overstimulated, tense and under pressure he may be upset with accompanying problems in behavior or negative emotional reactions.

3. He expresses anger not uncommonly through physical violence of a small sort and through words or threats.

4. He is easily aroused to a feeling of sympathy.

5. He usually has a keen sense of humor. This differs from adult humor and needs to be understood as an expression of a young child's point of view.

## IV. Socially

1. A child, when he has a choice, usually will become a part of a group of from two to five. Few will continue week after week in solitary activities, and few will choose voluntarily a group of more than five children. Each will select his own balance of solitary or small-group activity if left free to choose.

2. The child is eager to learn better ways of building relationships and working out problems. He makes great strides in the "social arts" from four to six.

3. The child is very responsive to the attitudes of the leader.

## V. In Relation to Others

Each child has his own rate of developing. His own experiences and his own individual self have made him a distinct personality, unlike any other child, one for whom God cares deeply, and who can be led into fellowship with him.

# FROM FOUR TO SIX

## Therefore, leaders will do this:

7. Present ideas through the child's interests. Avoid symbolism and concepts of time and space as the basis for understanding new ideas.

## III. Emotionally

1. Establish a sequence of activities to help children to feel secure. Within the sequence, keep great flexibility and variety. Provide dependable places for children to find materials, and when there is a change in location, or in activity sequence, explain it simply to everyone.

2. Keep the voice pleasant and well-modulated. Have the room treated acoustically to allow work and play without either "shushing" or excessive noise. Anticipate and avoid situations which might create pressure for individuals or groups.

3. Accept occasional emotional outbursts with a matter-of-fact attitude and seek to discover the cause.

4. Be alert to develop in him feelings of kindness and concern.

5. Use wisely his sense of humor to get over many a rough spot and to develop a sense of rapport in the group.

## IV. Socially

1. Provide for much of the learning in the kindergarten to be done in small and flexible groups. Give children considerable freedom in choosing where to sit, with whom to play, and how to group themselves. Encourage the children to develop friendships and enjoy working and playing with others.

2. Be constantly aware of the attitudes which the behavior of individuals toward others indicates. Seek to help each child to find Christian ways of working and playing with others, making sure that these spring from a growing thoughtfulness and consideration for the feelings and happiness of others.

3. Be kind and fair, without showing favoritism in the group. Seek to help the group to appreciate each member of the kindergarten and to help one another. Make the kindergarten itself a laboratory in Christian living.

## V. In Relation to Others

Accept each child as a person and avoid comparisons with other children. Know him, pray for him, visit his home, show a personal interest in him, try to help him to grow in Christian ways.

defined, and we must work with him and with his laws if we are to teach effectively. We cannot hope to impart a complete Christian education at this age. Therefore, we have tried to discover how we can adequately present Christian truth to meet the child's everyday needs at this age and to establish strong foundations on which continuing development can take place in years to come.

To help us to think clearly about these objectives, they are presented in six areas, although we are aware that these areas are interrelated and overlapping. The objectives should be as clearly a part of the teacher's thinking as the characteristics of the child. The specific goals which lead to fulfilling the objectives are given at the beginning of every session in all teacher's guides to week by week planning. Let us seek to know our objectives as they relate to the kindergarten child. To help us master these, suppose we study each area of the objectives and list the ideas, feelings, and actions we hope will grow out of the child's kindergarten experience.

## THE CHILD AND GOD

| What "ideas" (about God) do we seek to establish at this age? | What "feelings" (toward God) do we seek to establish at this age? | In what "actions" should these thoughts and feelings culminate? |
|---|---|---|
| God loves me and cares for me.<br>God has created this wonderful world.<br>God is wise and real and important.<br>God wants my love and wants me to do right.<br>God wants me to talk with him; to think about him.<br>God loves all people.<br>God is interested in my everyday experiences.<br>God will always help me. | Love for God<br>Appreciation for his love and kindness<br>Wonder at his marvelous world<br>Desire to know more about him<br>Satisfaction in working with him and for him<br>Freedom in talking with him<br>Joy in moments of worship | Expressing thanks to God<br>Talking with God<br>Working with God in simple ways<br>Asking questions about God<br>Singing praises to God<br>Doing friendly things for others |

# THE CHILD AND JESUS

### Ideas

God sent Jesus as a baby.
Jesus was a kind and loving person.
Jesus taught and showed what God is like.
God wants us to live the way Jesus taught.
Jesus is my Friend.
The Bible tells about Jesus.

### Feelings

Love for Jesus
Beginning appreciation for his life and teachings
Desire to carry out simple teachings of Jesus and to be like him
Enjoyment of the stories of Jesus
Thankfulness to God for Jesus
Desire to share stories of Jesus with other children

### Actions

Doing friendly things for others
Thanking God for Jesus
Bringing gifts to make it possible to share the story of Jesus

# THE CHILD AND THE BIBLE

### Ideas

The Bible is a special book.
It tells about God and Jesus.
It tells us how to live.
It has interesting stories.
It has verses to learn.
Parents and teachers love the Bible.

### Feelings

Interest in its contents
Enjoyment of stories
Appreciation of meaningful verses
Desire to carry out its directions
Desire to share it with others

### Actions

Learning Bible verses
Handling the Bible carefully
Using some simple Bible truths in everyday living

# THE CHILD AND THE CHURCH

### Ideas

The church is a special place.
Children and grownups find friends in the church.
At church we learn about God, Jesus, the Bible and ourselves.
There is a place in the church for me.
Many people work to make the church what it is.
I can help in my church too.
People everywhere need churches.

### Feelings

Love for the church
Joy in fellowship and in experiences there
Desire to share in its work
Appreciation for the work of the church and for the people in it
Friendliness toward the minister, the caretaker and other helpers

### Actions

Co-operation in good use of building and equipment
Sharing in work projects
Bringing gifts for the work of the church
Inviting friends to come too
Attend as much as possible

## RELATIONSHIP TO OTHERS AND PERSONAL GROWTH

| Ideas | Feelings | Actions |
|---|---|---|
| God wants me to grow. | Love for other people | Playing happily with others |
| God is concerned about me. | Desire to act in God's way | Working happily with others |
| What I do affects others. | Confidence in God's love, in his concern that I be an upright person | Talking with God about my interests |
| I can do many things for others. | | Asking God's help for right living |
| I can do many things for myself. | Appreciation for the contributions of others to happy living | Sharing with the world family |
| God will help me to do right. | | Doing helpful things at home |

## MOVING TOWARD OBJECTIVES

When we know the child and we have our objectives clearly in mind, we are ready to move in the direction of achieving our goals. This can never be done by vague generalities, but must be done by offering the child specific experiences which will spontaneously interest him and will help to bring about growth. Only an activity which will contribute toward the child's Christian growth in ideas, feelings or actions may justifiably be included in the church kindergarten program. We might also remind ourselves that the manner in which an activity is offered to the children and the way in which it is carried on have a strong bearing on the degree of its effectiveness in achieving goals.

Let us suppose that on a mild fall day the kindergarten group is taking a walk around the outside of the church for the purpose of looking at windows and doors, the roof and the chimney, noticing which windows are for the sanctuary, which for the kitchen, which for the "class for daddies and mommies," and which let light into the room where big brothers and sisters are thinking of God.

Suddenly Alan spies a nice furry black and brown caterpillar moving along through the grass. In that moment the church is forgotten as all the children clamor for a closer look and even to touch him. Knowing the kindergarten child and knowing the objectives, the teacher sees an opportunity and remembers these words: "As he enjoys the world about him we will lead him to think more directly of God as the Creator of this wonderful world and to feel a sense of belonging to it." As this idea flashes through the teacher's mind he is already speaking: "Did you know that God made the caterpillar and planned for him to turn into a butterfly? Perhaps if we take him into our room and put him in a jar with some grass and leaves, Mr. Caterpillar will spin a cocoon," the teacher suggests.

Back in the room with the caterpillar safely in the glass jar and lumbering up the twigs the children have placed there for him, the teacher says, "Let's talk with God about the wonderful caterpillar we found while we were walking outside the church!" He bows his head and prays briefly, "We are glad we found the caterpillar, O God. It makes us stop and think how wonderful you are because you planned for such creatures. Thank you for our church where all of us, grownups and children, can come to learn about you. Amen."

In this simple incident children may have experienced growth toward these other objectives:

"to feel that he can talk with God naturally about his interests, for God wants to hear the things that make the child glad,"

"to feel a sense of fellowship with God who is still actively at work in his world,"

"to feel a love for God that finds expression in joyous worship,"

"to think of the church as a special place where families . . . learn more about God."

None of these objectives is totally reached in one such simple experience, but every such experience strengthens the child's thinking and feeling and helps to establish within him Christian attitudes and ideas.

## OBJECTIVES AND OURSELVES

As you read the objectives, you will note a number of references to parents' and teachers' attitudes and to their effect upon the children's growth. We cannot escape the fact that children of four to six are great "copiers." They copy our tones of voice and activities; they dress up and pretend to be *us;* they repeat our comments word for word and do the things we do. They have an uncanny ability to "see through" us and to know whether we ring true.

Knowing children, we must know that our personal convictions as we live them will have a tremendous influence on the effectiveness of our teaching. This would be an overwhelming realization if we were not sure that God, who has called us to serve him by teaching, invites us into a daily growing relationship with himself, and will give us abundantly the help that we need.

---

"Our God, we give thanks for the wonder of the patterns of growth which thou hast established. Open our understanding as we seek to know how young children feel and think and act. Give us a clear view of our purposes as we prepare to guide the children, and help us to grow personally in our relationship with thee as each day of our life comes and goes. Amen."

---

### Projects and Discussion Questions

1. Discuss: How will knowing the children influence your behavior as their teacher?
2. Observe a kindergarten group. What characteristics do they display? What feelings were experienced by teacher and children? Refer to chart on pages 22-25.
3. Select one kindergarten child and study his behavior. In what ways does he seem to act in a manner characteristic of his age level? In what ways does he seem to be mature or immature for his chronological age?
4. Give specific examples of the ways a child's behavior might vary in church kindergarten because of some special situation or circumstance at home.
5. Mention one type of behavior which may cause problems in the kindergarten. Give ten possible reasons for this behavior.
6. Why is it important to know what behavior is typical of the four-to-six-year-old child? Why is it important further to know how individuals vary from the pattern?

CHAPTER 2

# LIVING WITH CHILDREN AT CHURCH

## LET'S START WITH YOU

Let's start with you, since the most important factor in the picture is the teacher — more important than the room, the equipment, the length of the session, the size of the group, or anything else! An educator once said, "You can have a good school in a hole in the wall if you have the right teacher." We are sure you will have a better place to work than "a hole in the wall," but if space is inadequate, the "right teacher" will do something about it.

So let's start with *you*. How do you look? Children appreciate attractiveness, and all teachers, men and women, can have some of this. A becoming hair style, good grooming, a dash of bright color, simple clothes; these things delight the young child. Dress with the child's interests in mind — simply, but with touches of variety. And women, *take off your hats,* even if they are very becoming ones!

How do you feel? Teaching kindergarten calls for you to be at your best. This means an alert, rested body; a relaxed, poised spirit; and a ready mind. Contributing factors will be adequate preparation through background knowledge of children and materials, and through specific planning for the session at hand. Also important are sufficient rest the night before, arriving at church well ahead of the children, prayer before the session, and an awareness of God's guiding and supporting presence.

To give yourself the advantage of attractive appearance and a maximum of readiness is to be well on the way toward a happy experience in living with children at church in the kindergarten room.

## SUNDAY IS LIKE THIS

What is Sunday like in the good church kindergarten? It is not a grownups' class on a reduced scale in which the children come in, take their places, and sit as quietly as the teacher can make them, listening to the words of wisdom she dispenses for their enlightenment. It is not merely a play period in which children find one interesting play activity after another, following entirely their own whims and fancies and just "enjoying" a busy morning as they wish. It is not a "busywork" session, in which the teacher stakes off required pieces of handwork which the children must take home finished to suit adult standards (and, frequently, largely executed by the teacher). It *is* a carefully planned session in which the teacher guides the group into a series of activities, each having its own purpose and related to the main idea of the session. It includes elements of listening, of play, of work, of worship, of contributing ideas, of expressing with materials and words the feelings and thoughts which have been gained during the session. It has been planned not with the idea of conveying a body of facts to the child to be known and repeated back parrot-fashion, but with the belief that, working with God's laws of growth, we can offer the child experiences on his level of interest and ability which will help him to develop Christian thoughts and feelings resulting in Christian behavior.

### In the One-Hour Session

The one-hour session may have a sequence of four major activity-groupings. There is first the *Informal Time* of about twenty minutes. During this time children arrive, remove outdoor clothing, greet friends, look at new things in the room, place offering in the basket, and make their own choice of the activities being offered in the various interest centers in the room (see page 57). These might include, in a session on helping at home, such activities as looking at pictures of homes and families in storybooks, building houses out of blocks, dramatizing family activities in the housekeeping corner, making crayon pictures of our families, watering the plants. As the end of this Informal Time approaches, the teacher tells the children it is time to "put away," and the room is made neat as each child shares in putting into order the area in which he has been busy.

Then there is *Together Time*. The characteristic of this block of time is that it includes activities in which the whole group can share simultaneously. The group usually gathers in the same area of the room each week, facing a center where there is a low table with a picture, the offering basket, and a Bible. The group may be seated informally on the floor, or on chairs, with the teacher seated facing them. Here they discuss the things they have been doing since they came into the room, sing together, pray, listen to a story, enjoy verses from the Bible or a picture, discuss some question which is related to the session's purpose. The teacher tries to include in this block of time some of the main ideas about which she wants children to think in this particular session, and to encourage them to think for themselves along lines related to the session. She (or he) stimulates their thinking and feeling by the materials she includes for their participation and consideration; these materials have been planned ahead of time (the songs, the story, the pictures, the Bible verses), but she is ready to change their order, or to add or subtract as she feels the flow of group interest. When the group tends to get "off the track" the teacher tactfully draws their interest back — unless, as sometimes happens, she wisely recognizes that there are greater values in following the children's direction than the one which she had planned!

The third major activity-grouping consists of *Creative Activities*. Here children are encouraged to express in words; in drama; in music; or with crayons, scissors, and paste, some of the thoughts and feelings which have been initiated or strengthened through their experiences in this session. This might take the form of freehand drawing, of making up a song or story, of planning a service project, of playing the story, of dictating a letter inviting a visitor to tell us about our church, or his work. Again the direction of this activity is determined by the theme of the session. About twenty minutes of the session is used for this type of activity.

The last block of time is short and is given to the preparation for going home; it is the *Closing Moments*. Though short, it is a very important part of the session. It needs careful planning so that there will not be "a lot of loose ends" and a grand confusion. It may include a song related to what we have been doing, a verse we have used earlier in the session, a reminder of something to be done at home, making sure children have work and belongings to take home, and a personal good-by between friends as the children go. This part of the session, as the first three do, will vary from Sunday to Sunday and will relate to the main ideas of the session. Gone forever is the plan of singing the same "'good-by song" every week, year in and year out. Closing moments can be *meaningful* instead.

### In the Two-Hour Session

The two-hour session will follow the same general sequence as the one-hour session; the major differences will be that more time can be allowed for each activity and that there can be a *Relaxation Time*. Looking more closely at the two-hour session we observe that a few very desirable characteristics may be added to each block of time designated for the one-hour session.

During the *Informal Time*, children may have more nearly thirty than twenty minutes to use. They may therefore: (1) complete one activity, then go to another, (2) spend a greater length of time in one activity, satisfying their own wishes to develop the activity further or in a more leisurely fashion, or (3) carry out an activity which requires a longer time and therefore cannot be included in the shorter session. Such longer activities might be: a walk to a nearby garden, making a frieze, painting, enjoying reels of a Viewmaster, making blueprints.

During the *Together Time* children will not be kept sitting any longer at one stretch than in the shorter session, for most four- and five-year-olds cannot sit more than ten minutes and continue to learn. We can, however, provide a richer assortment of activities here in the longer time available, thus adding to the effectiveness of the child's learning. Frequently a dramatization, additional music experiences, or an additional discussion time in which more children have turns to share can be included.

The *Relaxation Time* gives opportunity for teaching the habit of grace before food, enables children to assume some responsibility for helping to serve the food and clean up, offers time for an additional story, gives a change of pace through a snack and rest (at least 15 minutes) which permits better learning, and makes it possible for children to have more time to put into practice under supervision some of the Christian principles of living together. Such opportunities make the two-hour session distinctly advantageous. Perhaps it should be said here again that activities for this block of time are also definitely planned to strengthen the purposes of the session and carry them forward to realization. The rest period is discussed further on pages 75-77.

*Creative Activities* in the longer session may include more activities than are included in the one-hour session. Frequently, however, the longer time simply permits the child to work longer, and more thoroughly.

*Closing Moments* are allowed more nearly ten than five minutes when we have the two-hour session. This gives encouragement to more deliberate motion at dismissal time, and tends to cut down the feeling of pressure or hurry that is so easy to accept as necessary when parents are arriving to pick up children. Some of this excitement can be eliminated by posting a teacher at the door to call the children as the parents arrive. The more relaxed dismissal is sure to be the happier experience for everyone concerned.

## EQUIPPING TO MEET THEIR NEEDS[1]

Once upon a time, the "beginners" class could meet in the kitchen, the Ladies Aid room, or the corner of the sanctuary opposite the choir simply by the procedure of adding little chairs in sufficient numbers to accommodate the "little ones."

Church school teaching must still go on in many improvised spaces, and this will continue to be true with the strong upswing in population in most localities and the pressing need for church school rooms. Adapting a space for good

[1] For further information, see *Our Church Plans for Children*, Blankenship, Chapter 6, "Space and Equipment."

kindergarten teaching is no longer a simple proposition. We cannot always provide the ideal equipment and the ideal space, but we must keep on striving toward the ideal. We must look creatively at what we have to work with, and work creatively until we have equipped our space adequately for good kindergarten teaching.

Let us look at the ideal and refuse to accept the notion that the ideal cannot become a reality in our local situation. It is amazing what can be done to achieve the ideal when a teacher knows what is needed and why, and is able to arouse the interest of parents and staff members in providing a well-equipped room for the kindergarten!

## Work Area

Children need a work surface at a convenient height, well lighted. They need seating which has a comfortable relationship to the work surface. (Have *you* ever tried to write on a table at shoulder height, or work at a table under which you could scarcely squeeze your knees?) The size of the table is flexible, but tables should seat at least six for comfortable work. This means a width of 24 to 36 inches, a length of three feet. Height should be 22" for use with chairs of 12" height (10" higher than the chairs). When floor space is at a premium, it is better to sacrifice some table space in order to have space for activities and other equipment. It is possible to improvise for work space, using the floor or staggering the use of tables timewise.

Tables should be easily movable to allow for a flexible arrangement in the room, and flexible seating at the tables. Surfaces will need to be smooth and to be neither dark nor glaring white. A natural wood or a Masonite top finish is ideal, for this will offer no sharp contrast to any work children do and, therefore, no eye strain. If paint or a self-adhesive plastic surface is used, the color should have an intensity of about the same quality as natural wood.

Also important is adjacent space within the child's easy vision and reach for supplies which children need when they work. Here, too, should be a wastebasket and a dustpan and brush to encourage the children to clean up. Children are able to get the things they need by themselves.

### The Block Area

A block shelf on which to store unit blocks, sets of wooden animals and people, cars and trucks and Masonite squares or rectangles, should be adjacent to a floor space adequate for the building projects of three or four children. If your space is very limited, you might have to settle for a box of blocks. Four-year-olds sometimes find a box somewhat more inviting for blocks than shelves, perhaps because the putting-away job is easier. The writer has discovered that the "fives" find putting blocks away intriguing if red shapes are pasted on the back of the shelf where each size and shape is to go.

Large hollow wooden blocks or cardboard blocks are excellent for quick construction of large buildings or vehicles in which children can engage in dramatic play.

### The Music Area

If there is enough space in the room, a piano is desirable, though it is not essential if the teacher will become skilled in the use of other resources — her own voice, the record player, a xylophone or autoharp, and rhythm instruments. Instruments may be kept on a shelf or arranged on an easily accessible peg-board; rhythm sticks, bells, jingle-clogs, drums, and sand blocks may be purchased or homemade, but triangles will have to be purchased as will tambourines, if these are desired. A few good basic rhythm records and resting records should be stored in a rack with a plastic cover or in albums. A pair of bookends and three or four good song books will complete the music equipment.

### Housekeeping Area

Separated from the rest of the room by a low screen which may or may not be painted to look like the outside of a house, is the housekeeping corner equipped with furnishings to encourage the dramatic play of many activities which children see going on in their own homes. The part of this area which represents the kitchen will be furnished with a child-size table and chairs, stove, sink, and dish cupboard together with other tools and equipment which make up an efficient kitchen. A chest of drawers for doll clothes and bedding and many other household items may be added as desired.

### Book Area

Needed in the kindergarten room is a shelf on which are arranged a selection of picture books chosen with the child's Christian growth in mind. Books must be invitingly arranged on the shelf standing, so that children can easily see the front cover as they make a choice. A table, preferably round, and chairs may be allocated to this area to encourage browsing. Suggestions for books for this area will be found throughout teaching materials and in Christian education magazines. Be sure to include on the bookshelf copies of the pupil's book from your kindergarten course.

### Open Floor Space

One important feature of the kindergarten room is an area of open floor space. This is needed not only to give the room an uncluttered and restful atmosphere, but to provide for unobstructed programming. Many activities call for space in which children can gather as a group to sit or to move about freely. The piano, if there is one, should be adjacent to the open floor space since both music activities and the Together Time (during which the piano may be used) require a cleared area. Nearby, too, should be a low table holding an open Bible, an offering basket, flowers, and a special picture, chosen for that particular session. The wall clock should be visible from the teacher's place as she sits near the low table.

### Storage Space

Some provision must be made for a place to keep the children's work as well as their outdoor clothing. Individual lockers, or "cubbies," are the best solution to this problem. With hooks at the child's convenient level and a shelf for work, mittens, pocketbook, hat, and other small belongings, "cubbies" permit the child to keep his own belongings in a place he feels is his own. Each section can be marked with a small card, 1"x3", on which the child's name is neatly printed and on which an identifying object (a ball, wagon, apple, etc.) has been placed also, since few children recognize their names when they first attend kindergarten. Gummed stickers, each different, also may be used on these "cubby tags." If necessary, three children may use one cubby by placing identification on the three sides. It is important to keep such equipment portable so that the room can be rearranged as desired. If it is not possible to have individual lockers, use a portable coat rack with a rod 36″ from the floor, with hangers for wraps.

Shelf units for children's work materials should also be easily movable. If you cannot have wooden shelves, you can use gaily painted orange crates (if you can obtain them) or even sturdy cardboard grocery cartons, stacked sideways and secured into a unit by the use of long, heavy paper fasteners.

For the teachers' materials a closet or stock room adjacent to the kindergarten room is ideal, but many teachers will have to settle for a shelf or shelves in the room. These shelves should have doors, preferably sliding ones.

### For Relaxation Time

Increasingly, church schools are providing a low utility sink as part of the kindergarten's basic equipment. Otherwise, a bucket of water and sponges will be needed in every room.

Needed for the lunch time are a tray, paper or plastic cups, napkins, and a pitcher, baskets for passing cookies, crackers, fruit, or carrot sticks, and a metal can with a tight lid for storing crackers.

For rest, each child will need a small washable rug or bath towel his size, which he can bring from home and leave at church. The church may provide mats or cots.

## A WORD ABOUT ARRANGEMENT

The attractiveness and usefulness of the kindergarten will be determined to a large extent by the arrangement of the equipment. All equipment should be movable, so that you can look critically at the room occasionally to see whether it is serving your purposes with maximum efficiency.

Important principles brought out in the discussion above may well be summarized in the following check list. Apply these to your own teaching space periodically.

1. Furniture is grouped to create the following areas:
    (a) an open floor space

    (b) a work space where light is good and materials conveniently at hand
    (c) a place for building with blocks
    (d) a housekeeping center
    (e) a place for enjoying books
    (f) a good location for Together Time where children will not be facing a window or an entrance door
    (g) storage space for outdoor clothing, easily accessible
2. Ventilation is adequate and does not create a direct draft on children grouped for activities in any area.
3. Lighting is adequate and is especially good in work space and book areas, as well as on pictures.
4. Floor is unobstructed near doors. Block and housekeeping areas are away from the flow of traffic.
5. Equipment used together is kept together — records near the record player, work shelves near work tables, rhythm instruments near the piano, and so forth.
6. Piano is placed so teacher using it can see group. It is not placed directly against a heating unit.
7. Facilities for washing and toileting are nearby.

## TOWARD THE IDEAL

Consider the resources at hand for bringing your kindergarten facilities more nearly into line with the ideal. An analysis of your needs, plus a creative approach to meeting them is sure to produce changes toward the ideal. Parents will respond to a well-planned program for improving the kindergarten room, and may be enlisted for a work party with all materials on hand, a job for everybody, enthusiasm and a coffee break. Individuals will respond to an invitation to make or repair a specific piece of equipment at home if you select the job to suit the interests of the parents. Catalogs from equipment companies will frequently furnish ideas and specifications for good additions to your room (see bibliography). Occasionally the purchase of a new piece of equipment may become a special project for some adult group within the church fellowship. Each year the Christian education budget of the church should include provision to add some equipment to the kindergarten. The leader's responsibility is to know what is needed and why; then, with patience, to take steps toward the ideal.

## IN THE SMALLER CHURCH

The smaller church offers the kindergarten teacher a challenge and an opportunity. She may find that instead of a room of her own she must share a room with other age groups and only a corner of it is hers to equip to meet the needs of the kindergarten children. But knowing the ideal, and being personally equipped with love, patience, determination, and ingenuity, she can still do an excellent teaching job. The most important factor is still the teacher who knows the child and his needs, who knows God personally, and who constantly seeks the best teaching methods. Whether the church is small or large, this factor does not change. The challenge comes in adapting teaching suggestions to the space in which this teacher must work.

Informal time will need to be held when the other groups are singing; relaxation time when the others are quiet, and so forth. Activities and interest groups will be fewer. The floor will need to be used for work space (or lapboards).

You can still have a good program in spite of limitations. And when weather is nice, you may be able to have your session outside.

Every child is important and no group is too small to deserve the best. Good teachers have found they can do a good job in almost any situation while they are working to improve teaching conditions.

## GROUPING

A better teaching job can be done when it is possible to have two separate rooms for the two age groups. The four-year-old group (Kindergarten I) is but a small step up from the Nursery Department with a program which develops with the children. The five-year-old group (Kindergarten II), built on Kindergarten I, bridges the gap toward first grade and offers a continuing challenge to the child's interest. When separate rooms are not available and the kindergarten attendance reaches eighteen to twenty, it may be wise to have two groups within the same room for Together Time.

Within the room, grouping is "fluid." During Informal Time each child becomes a part of a small group, busy with some common interest. When teachers notice a child remaining an individual apart from the groups it is their responsibility to help that child to find a satisfying place as a member of a small group, or at least to become one of a partnership. A teacher makes a place for the child in the small group by suggesting some way in which his help is needed, some special project of which he may become an immediate part, some interest he has in common with another child, or a special way a member of the group may show friendliness to him. From the small groups of Informal Time children move into the larger group for Together Time, then into smaller groups again for washing, lunch, and rest (in the longer session), and for Creative Activities. The grouping thus flows from one formation to another, and in the teacher's handling of these transitions lies much of the secret of a smoothly moving kindergarten.

Some teachers have used the plan of dividing the kindergarten into "families" to facilitate transitions and supervision during small group activities. When this plan is followed, children are divided into groups of five or six and each group is given the name of a bird, flower, animal, or the name of the teacher responsible for each group. Or, the children may want to name their own family. Such small groups within the larger group give children a feeling of security and provide opportunity for children to express themselves more freely. Small groups also help the teachers to get acquainted with each child more quickly. Another device for moving the group to a new activity is to place a stand-up marker (an animal or flower) in the middle of each table and refer to this when instructing a group.

When children are in a large group teachers sometimes find it helpful to facilitate a transition to a new grouping by suggesting, "All the people with blue on may stand up. They may go to their table and begin work." Other children may look at a picture together or sing a song together so that a minute or two passes before the teacher calls the next children to get their books. Kindergarten children tend to stampede when a teacher tries to move everyone at once.

Grouping is important for accomplishing the work of the kindergarten effectively. Alert teachers will soon observe that some combinations of children are much more congenial than others. Jim and Jeff get into a scuffle whenever they are together; Sue and Linda "chit-chat" straight through everything when they sit next to each other; while Clark and Bill are a bad combination because one depends on the other for everything. When these situations become apparent, the wise teacher will place these children in different groups most of the time, so that each may develop better and not disrupt the whole group.

Factors in grouping, then, are chronological age, space available, number of teachers, activities in progress, and individual personalities.

## KEEPING RECORDS

There is no substitute for accurate and adequate records in the kindergarten. It is simply impossible for the teacher's memory to retain many of the things discovered while teaching, or to keep in mind an awareness of the many facts about each child which help in accomplishing the most effective work. Records, therefore, must be well kept and they must always be available. Finally, they must be *used* to be of value.

From the time a child first attends as a visitor until the time he leaves the department, every record should be kept conscientiously. It may seem strange but it is a fact that an inaccurate record can do much to cancel the effectiveness of a teacher's work. Alan comes as a visitor; nobody knows his last name or nobody remembers his address, nobody follows through. He likes church school, but his family doesn't bother, so he doesn't come back. Randy is absent three Sundays in a row, but no one notices because there is still a "good attendance." It happens that Randy is in the hospital with pneumonia. Here the church has missed an opportunity to be friendly and to reach a pair of very receptive parents. Pam's birthday comes and goes and her church school teacher doesn't even know it! And what a big event a birthday is to a five-year-old!

Secure your denominational record system and see that it is accurately kept.

### Group Lists

Each teacher should have a list of all the children for whom he is responsible, with complete information on each child.

### Birthday List

A list of birthdays in calendar order should be placed on the wall for the teachers' easy reference. This may be typed and mounted neatly. Another method of keeping this record is to write children's names in on a calendar at the correct date. Be sure the child receives a birthday card or telephone call on his "special day," and that he is recognized in some way (*not* with a disappointing *wooden* birthday cake) in the session nearest his birthday.

### Records and Your Pastor

When your records show a fact which would be helpful to your pastor or church office, make a note of it *in writing* and give it to the pastor or church secretary.

"Alan James has moved to Chicago. A new family has bought his house at 603 Walnut Street." This note may result in a new family becoming interested in your church, if you get it to the pastor promptly. Or the church may be able to serve a real need if the pastor knows that "Keith Phillips was absent because his mother broke her arm." The kindergarten *is* part of the total church fellowship.

---

Our God, we give thanks for the privilege of living with boys and girls at church. Help us to look searchingly at ourselves and at the rooms in which we work to see whether they and we measure up to the best — for only the best is worthy of thee. Grant us creative vision and determined energy to make what is good better, and to give attention to the small details which will make our teaching more effective. These things we pray that we may be used to bring each child into fellowship with thee. Amen.

## Projects and Discussion Questions

1. What four major blocks of time may be included in the kindergarten session?
   What is the major role of each? What activities may be included in each?
2. Describe one of the following areas in a kindergarten room with which you are acquainted: work area; block area; housekeeping area; music area; book area; storage space; open floor space; facilities for washing and toileting. How could the area you have described be brought nearer the ideal?
3. Make up a scale based on the check list on pages 39-40. Allow points for each requirement adding up to a total of 100. Then rate the kindergarten in your local church on its facilities.
4. Plan one improvement in the kindergarten room, or space, of your church and carry out your plans.
5. Observe a kindergarten session. List in order the various types of groupings employed. What factors influenced the groupings? How did the leading teacher get children from one grouping to another?
6. Describe in detail the records which now are in use at your church kindergarten? How would you rate the method in which they are kept? Consult a church school or stationer's supply catalog and make an order list for supplies needed to complete the kindergarten records. Submit this to the kindergarten superintendent for possible use.

CHAPTER 3

# KNOWING AND USING CURRICULUM MATERIALS

The children who come into the kindergarten on Sunday mornings have a wider knowledge of people, events, and facts than the grade school child of a generation ago. True, the knowledge may be spotty and some of the information may be inaccurately remembered, but the four-to-six-year-old's fund of information is rather startling. As a matter of fact, he is quite likely to be well informed about some things which his teacher does not know. He has a very absorbent mind and he is exposed every day to vivid audio and visual impressions.

All this adds up to the fact that the teacher must make the material live; it must captivate the children's interest. It will do so only if he knows what he is doing. There can be no substitute for thorough preparation. Such preparation requires knowing the curriculum materials to be used in the kindergarten, then preparing for an approaching unit, and preparing for each specific session.

## KNOWING THE MATERIAL

Secure a complete set of the materials used in your church kindergarten and examine them, piece by piece. You will find that they include material for the children and material for the parents as well as material for the teacher. It is important for you to know what parents' and children's materials contain as well as what is in the teacher's material. Take time to become thoroughly familiar with each piece of material. This will mean knowing each picture in the sets provided.

Then turn to the recommended book of songs. Why do you think children will like these songs? As you read over the words, you will discover that each song is closely related to the child's experience. Select a few that you like best and learn them; sing them over in moments when you are not preoccupied during the week, so that they come to you easily. If a recording of the songs is available, listen to the songs until they become "yours." Become familiar with the table of contents, the subjects included and the way songs are arranged.

Look over the parents' materials. What kind of suggestions do they contain? Some teachers find it helpful to paste the parents' material just inside the cover of the teacher's book for the same quarter so that they can easily refer back and forth from one to the other. Parents and teachers are a team and as you are aware of the home suggestions in your curriculum materials you will be better able to work with parents for the Christian growth of their children week by week.

Next look at the pupil's materials. As you read story materials you will discover what vocabulary and what kind of sentence is needed to make meanings clear to the kindergartener. As you look over materials to be used for the child's activities, you will discover what type of activities appeal to the kindergartener, and how simple they must be to be successfully accomplished by him.

The teacher's book contains such a wealth of material that you may feel a moment of consternation: "How can I ever put so much material to use? I don't know where to begin!" A closer look should offer you reassurance. Here is a complete handbook to help you. You are not a servant to this book; instead, it is a servant to you! The suggestions are in forms that are easily understood — in diagrams, in outlines, in boxes, in pictures. The type is easy to read. All you need to do in order to "find your way around" easily in this teacher's book is to spend some time discovering what is there. It's like opening packages for Christmas; every bit of investigating turns up something else that you can use. Like Christmas gifts too, there will be some things you'll need and like, and put to work immediately. Some of the other things you will be glad to know are there to use when you will need them later on!

## PREPARING FOR A UNIT

Now that the preliminaries are over, it is time to get down to the planning stages. Here is the curriculum material, there in the kindergarten room you can visualize your group. How can you translate these printed things into activities that will captivate those eager boys and girls and help them to grow in Christian ways? It takes just one step at a time, until there you are, ready to teach!

The children who come in will "see" only the activities, not the purposes or the units — the overall picture that the teacher sees on which the activities are established. Units are the framework in which individual sessions are placed. They give the sessions relation to one another as the rooms in the house go together to make up the home. Each session makes its own contribution to the unit and builds toward a total effect. Before we can plan well for a session, we must plan for the unit. This unit planning should be done with other members of the kindergarten staff at meetings held monthly or quarterly. The superintendent or leading teacher (may be one and the same) will take the initiative in such planning (see page 103). Steps in this preparation may be as follows:

1. Become familiar with the title of the unit and with the session titles included in that unit by examining the Table of Contents.

2. Find out why this unit is offered by reading the introduction to the unit and studying the unit purpose. Think through the relation of the unit to the objectives of Christian education of kindergarten children.

3. Read the list of major activities and mark them with a bracket. Note the page so you can easily refer back to it.

4. Look at the unit outline. Do this with other curriculum materials spread out before you. Check to see if the pupil's book is to be used in any session. Lay out pictures mentioned in the outline. Make a note of the songs to be used in the unit. Examine activity material to be used.

5. In a prayerful spirit, read the session purposes.

6. With pencil in hand read the outline for each of the sessions of the unit, choosing from the activities suggested those most helpful in your situation. As you read, use a pencil to underline materials you are not certain are on hand, and to check activities for which you might need to plan more than one session ahead. (Refer to session plans for closer reading where you have a question.)

7. List on a slip of paper the materials you have underlined and make plans to secure them.

When your staff has taken these preliminary steps, learn the songs for the unit together. If a new procedure is suggested about which you are not sure, let a member of the staff demonstrate it. Do together a few selected activities which are suggested for the children. Choose one or two from each session of the unit. It will add tremendously to your feeling of familiarity with what is to come. Decide on any assignments which members of the staff are to carry out during the unit. "Eleanor has agreed to secure additional books from the town library and arrange the book area." "Grace will be responsible for the frieze in the second session, and the arrangements for the gift basket in later sessions." "I will be leading teacher this month and be responsible for the Together Time." Thus the responsibilities are summarized at the close of the planning meeting for the unit.

With this background, teachers can plan from week to week with only minor consultation between staff members, but the monthly meeting to do the overall unit planning is an essential for good work, even where there are only two members on the staff. (See page 103 for further reference to planning a unit.)

## PREPARING FOR A SESSION

How shall we go about planning for the session? These are the steps:

1. Read the entire session from the teacher's book.

2. Become familiar with stories, songs, and poems to be used in the session. Put markers in the Bible at verses to be used during the session. *Know these verses "by heart."*

3. Check to be sure all materials needed for the session are at hand.

4. Prepare special work materials if any are needed.

5. Check your teacher's material to make sure that you have taken care of all the suggestions for advance preparation. Check each suggestion with a pencil as you have completed it.

6. Read over the outline, visualizing the session in progress in your room. Make any adaptations which may contribute to a satisfying experience for the children.

7. Go to the kindergarten room early enough to have it ready for the arrival of the first child. Become aware of God's presence with you there as the children begin to come.

8. Be ready to use the children's ideas. Sometimes after the session has started you will change your carefully made plans in order to follow through a suggestion or idea of the children.

9. At the close of the session, begin to prepare for the next one by jotting down notes of things to be finished or remembered the following Sunday.

After all these specific directions it may be well to remind ourselves that preparation for all sessions goes on constantly. All personal growth, enjoyment of beauty, alertness to relationships, wonder and growing acquaintance with natural phenomena, deepening of the spiritual life, service to others, sense of closeness to God — all these prepare us for teaching a better session. Curriculum materials come alive only through the personality of you, the teacher.

The curriculum materials have been made very complete so that, using them correctly, together with your Bible, you are on the way to doing a good teaching job. Within the materials there are many helps for an effective kindergarten, concise statements dealing with specific aspects of the kindergarten program; you may wish to refer to these often. Use your table of contents freely and reread the brief discussions occasionally as a reminder and as a check on your procedure.

You may add further to the ongoing usefulness of your text if you will list on a blank page, cut to the size of your book, the page numbers of poems, rhythm plays, games, and prayers, which children especially enjoy. You then will be able to locate these easily for use at times other than where they are listed in your text. Paste the list along the binding of the inside cover at the back of the book. Children frequently ask again for an action song, for example, and it is good to be able to use materials again when children ask.

## SUPPLEMENTARY MATERIALS

Even though your curriculum materials are more than adequate, you will find it helpful to own a few good reference books (or see that they are available in your church library). A one-volume Bible commentary, a Bible atlas, and a Bible dictionary are good helps to own, purely from the point of view of enriching your own background.

You will also want to become acquainted with the professional magazines which deal with subjects and skills helpful for you to know. Your denomination provides a monthly publication which will help you in many ways to become a better teacher. Watch for book announcements of new publications in the kindergarten field. You will grow and add to your effectiveness as a teacher as you read the available new books.

## VISUAL MATERIALS

*Pictures.* Your curriculum materials have provided pictures which are ideal for kindergarten use. They are large, colorful, simple, and deal with subjects the child understands. They are authentic in detail and artistically good. You will want to file them by quarters so that you can always find them easily as their use is suggested in your text. If possible, it is helpful to have a second set of these pictures filed by subject.

In addition you will want to build a supplementary picture file. These you will choose from current magazines and from publicity materials of businesses, government agencies, and educational associations. Keep the same criteria of selection (pictures are to be large, colorful, simple, dealing with subjects in the child's experience, and relating to the purposes of church school sessions). Be especially alert for pictures with kindergarten appeal, of food, animals, children playing, family work and fun, seasonal activities, natural wonders. Pictures should be filed under simple classifications such as those mentioned in the preceding sentence. If not individually mounted, they should be kept flat by the use of cardboard dividers between sections. These should be cut the size of the largest pictures to protect edges and corners. Some teachers prefer not to mount pictures in the file, but to mount them as they are placed on bulletin boards. This may be done by using thumbtacks at the corners of the picture and through mounting sheets (such as construction paper) cut larger than the picture. (Thumbtacks may be placed close to the picture to hold it without going through the picture.) This enables the teacher to use one color of background sheets for the pictures on a single board or throughout the room for a unit. A color may be selected which suggests the season or the theme, but will be varied from unit to unit to add interest.

Pictures which have been mounted may be hung by using a piece of masking tape formed into a circle, sticky side out, and placed on the back of the picture. The tape will then stick to the picture and the wall without showing.

Another essential picture file is one that contains pictures which the children can use to paste on posters. These, too, should be filed by subject.

*Objects.* Provision should be made for the care and storage of nature materials, which can be used to enrich the curriculum again at some future time, as well as for objects relating to Bible life and to friends in other lands. Birds' nests, unusual shells, milkweed or wheat or barley stalks, coral, starfish, cocoons, and a poster showing vegetable seeds are the kinds of material worth saving. A good model of a Palestinian house, dolls dressed in Bible costumes or costumes of other lands, Japanese shoes, chopsticks, an Indian basket — these are things worth keeping since they may be used many times.

*Projected Pictures.* Projected pictures have a limited use in the kindergarten, but there is a place for occasional use of a few carefully chosen ones. A viewer or two and selected reels which deal with subjects such as forest animals, farm friends, children of other lands, or the seasons, for example, may be used on appropriate Sundays with very good results. A few filmstrips have been produced which are suitable for kindergarten children, and these would be worth the small investment involved just to have them available whenever you wish to use them. (Four or five times a year is often enough to show them.) Be sure to consult someone who *knows* before buying, however, or you will have wasted your money!

*Picture Books.* Although you may be able to borrow a few excellent books from your local library, your budget should provide for the addition of at least one new picture book for the kindergarten each quarter. Your curriculum materials list these, and you will find them listed also in resources provided annually by your denomination. Current prices, listed in the catalog, will enable you to plan your budget.

## HOW THE BIBLE IS USED

At first glance a new teacher may be unaware how completely the kindergarten curriculum is based upon the Bible. The use of the Bible in the kindergarten is based on the firm belief that the Bible should be to the child a familiar book, an important and beloved book which helps him to know how God wants him to live day by day. The curriculum is based on the further belief that the Bible can become all this to the child through using it in a number of ways.

1. The truths which the Bible teaches about God, the church, Jesus, our relationship to others and about the Book itself determine what is taught in the church kindergarten. Everything included in the session is measured according to its value in conveying to the child the Christian ideas, feelings, and spirit set forth in the Bible.

2. The Bible serves as the great resource for the teacher. In passages specifically suggested for each Sunday the teacher finds inspiration and direction for that particular session, as well as important background material essential to doing an adequate teaching job. This material is not shared directly with the child but provides a reservoir of spiritual experience without which any attempt at teaching is barren and unproductive.

3. The Bible serves as the source of all the stories used in the kindergarten; not only Bible stories as such but also the "everyday" stories. The latter are based on the Bible truths as mentioned in paragraph 1 in this section. These stories are expressed in terms the child can understand. They have

been carefully written to be accurate in biblical details, to take into consideration the Bible context and the Bible times in which they occurred. Stories are chosen in the light of the child's own experience and in the light of what will have significance for him. Since the Bible is an adult book, only part of the story material can be used with children. These Bible stories are selected carefully. Consideration is given to the fact that little children enjoy and need repetition and will sometimes gain more from hearing a story again than from hearing a new story. Even adults return to favorite passages of the Bible for inspiration and strength rather than always reading something new! Considering the limitations of time and the limitations of a four-to-six-year-old's understanding, it is amazing how much Bible story material is used, and how much variety of material is included.

4. Bible verses are used with the children with the purpose of making them meaningful in the lives of the children. This is done not through drill but through meaningful experiences in using the Bible verses. Verses for children to remember are set out at the beginning of each session for the teacher's special attention; then specific suggestions are included in the session plan about ways to use them. They are given emphasis by frequent use so that the child, retaining the words and ideas, may relate the verses to his experiences.

5. The Bible is kept in a special place in the room — an attractive place where children can see and handle it. Session plans call for the teacher to hold the Bible while she tells Bible stories; to give the children many occasions for holding it as verses are "read." Sometimes colored markers are placed at the location of a special story or verse to be used in a session. As a situation arises in which the teacher may refer to a verse or story meaningfully, she may go with a child to the Bible and show him where the verse or story is found. He will not be able to read the words, but he will enjoy knowing that "it is right there!"

## MOVING TOWARD ACCOMPLISHING OUR PURPOSES

Science has devised some phenomenal means of determining many factors but it is much more difficult to determine how completely we are achieving our purposes in the church school.

We cannot measure Christian growth as we can measure physical growth or growth in mental abilities. Nevertheless, it is important that we continually do our best to evaluate the results of our teaching. Preparation of the materials, the room, and ourselves is easily recognized as essential. But it is not easy to realize that a session is not really completed until we have looked at it critically to see what we can learn about its results.

It is a good idea to establish the habit of reviewing a session as soon as it is over and asking yourself the following questions:

1. Is there any way in which my room could have served the purposes of the session more adequately? Were there things I should have had ready or available which would have improved the session? Would some other arrangement of the room have been more satisfactory?

2. Were there any ways in which I myself should have been better prepared? Which parts of the session did not seem to "go over" well? Was this because I need to gain skill in handling this phase of the program, or because I didn't spend sufficient time in preparation to be sure of what I was doing? What part of the session went especially well? Why was this part superior?

3. Which of the purposes listed at the beginning of the session can I feel were accomplished? Read the purposes over and take time to think how each was achieved. What did the children say; what did they do? Did *every* child feel I was glad he was present? Did any problems of individual children come to light in the course of the session? (List these.) Were these completely solved or are there ways in which we can work on them further in succeeding sessions?

4. Make written notes *now* on suggestions for next Sunday. It will be helpful if members of the staff do the evaluating together. This may be done at the monthly staff meeting in which planning ahead takes place. Take a brief backward look first and use some of the questions above to guide you in your evaluation.

It is inevitable that you will improve as a teacher and find ways of doing more effective work, if you take the time to evaluate a session in the specific ways suggested above.

> We are grateful, our Father, for the planning and work of those who have prepared for us, with such care, the teaching materials that come to our hands. Help us to know that this is only a starting point for us, and help us to make these materials really our own as we use them in readiness to meet boys and girls. Give us insights and inspiration as we study and plan, and give us above all the certain knowledge that thy undergirding wisdom, thy vital presence, can add to our best efforts thy divine touch. Use us, O God, work through us, speak through us to the children we teach. We pray for these things with thankfulness for the privilege of sharing our faith with boys and girls. Amen.

## Projects and Discussion Questions

1. Study the songbook recommended for use with your course. What are the characteristics of the songs appearing there? Select five songs and decide which of the objectives listed on pages 6 to 10 is most closely related to each.

2. Working in groups of four or five class members, choose a unit of the kindergarten course and go about its preparation, preparing one session in detail. (See pages 48-49.) Report on your experience, raising questions or problems which have occurred as you worked.

3. With one or two others work on the picture file used by your church kindergarten, bringing it up to the desirable standard of usefulness.

4. Discuss the place of the Bible in the kindergarten. Use at least one supplementary source as a basis for the discussion.

CHAPTER 4

# HELPING CHILDREN TO LEARN

When we know what we want to accomplish with children, we still are faced with one absorbing question: How? What are some ways of teaching which have become accepted in the kindergarten because they have proven to be effective means of achieving our goals? New ways of effective teaching are constantly being discovered by teachers everywhere as they work with children. Once engaged in the business of teaching *you* will, as you gain experience, have the fun of discovering new ways of teaching. But, however little or much experience you have had, it will be helpful to you to learn how other teachers have helped children to learn.

## INTEREST GROUPS

An excellent way of involving children in the learning process is to offer a choice of interests and allow each to choose the one which appeals to him the most. These may vary from session to session in type as well as in content. Curriculum materials usually suggest several interest groups for each session, and also suggest specific ways in which the teacher may arrange and introduce these. Also frequently included in session plans are ideas for ways the teacher may guide the children in the interest groups.

An interest center is an area invitingly arranged for a definite activity. The teacher's first responsibility then, is to arrange the area before the session begins in such a way that children will be attracted to it. This means arranging work and play materials so that children may readily see possibilities for interesting participation and may be led into experiences which will stimulate thinking along the lines of the session's purposes.

*Preparation* of the interest centers is of major importance. As the teacher faithfully adds suggestive materials to various areas of the room week after week, children will begin to look for them, and, appreciating the fresh materials, enjoy carrying out activities with a slightly new slant. One week they find in the block corner a picture of a Palestinian house; there also are the paper stand-up figures of Joseph, Mary, and the boy Jesus. Another week they find a cardboard bell tower like the one on their own church — just waiting to have them build a church on which to mount it.

What could be done to prepare the housekeeping corner for a session in which the main idea is "Thanking God for Good Times at Home," or "Our Family Thanks God"? Knowing the title of the session would be sufficient to make a teacher ask this question, and come up with some good answers even before looking at the curriculum materials.

Two or three interest centers are to be found in the room every week but others are set up just for a specific session or two. A partial list of activities will serve to suggest the wide range of possibilities for which interest centers might be prepared: story-listening; making gifts; packing a basket with food gifts; playing a Bible story; enjoying picture books; making a large walk-in church of grocery cartons and a mattress box; examining leaves and seeds gathered in the fall; working puzzles of animals; caring for growing things; cutting out construction paper vegetables to put in an envelope-basket. Each of these will call for special *preparation* on the part of the teacher before the session begins.

But there are also other phases of the teacher's work, for as the children begin to use the interest centers, opportunities arise to observe how each is working. Is the purpose of the session getting across to him? What does his work indicate about his thinking? What is he discovering for himself? What has he found or done that is worth sharing with the group as a whole? How can the teacher, by a suggestion, further stimulate his creativity or enrich his experience?

In most situations the teacher needs to remain with the interest group to guide the activity, as in the case of playing a Bible story, or making a large-carton church. But in *all* situations the teacher's responsibility will include observation, interpretation, commendation, and suggestion.

The success of interest groups in helping children to learn is dependent upon the teacher's skill in preparing the interest centers, and in guiding the children in the centers. The teacher must know at what moments to encourage the child in his efforts, when and how to offer comments or guidance, at what moments to leave him alone, and how to use the child's experience for the growth of the group. This skill will come through study of curriculum materials, through observing other teachers at work with children in interest groups, and through practice week after week in setting up interest centers and guiding children in them.

## CONVERSATION

The exchange of ideas through conversation is a very important avenue of learning for every child. Such conversation may be carried out in a group or between two people. The atmosphere of the room is a key factor here, for children will share their ideas freely in conversation only when they themselves feel at ease in doing so; only when they know their ideas will be valued; and only as they are given opportunities to share.

This means that *children must feel at home* in the room and with the teacher and other children. The less outgoing ones will need practice in finding their ground as they talk with the teacher and other children individually before they will be ready to enter a conversation freely.

In a group conversation, seating will need to be sufficiently *informal* to suggest a free exchange of ideas. This does not necessarily mean a circle of chairs; children may easily sit on a rug on the floor. Groups will need to be *small* enough so that children will be able to contribute often instead of sitting a long time waiting for a turn to speak. The teacher will have to learn how to guide the conversation with a minimum of teacher-talking; children-listening pattern and a maximum of children-talking pattern. In this way children will have a real opportunity to share in group conversation.

Teachers will need to *maintain a balance* so that overeager children will not monopolize the conversation and overshy ones will not be embarrassed by being unable to come forth with a contribution. Watching the children's faces will usually give a cue to their readiness to participate. The way a teacher calls on even a shy child may give him confidence and make him forget himself in his eagerness to share an idea.

Conversation will be *stimulated* by good questions — questions which make children think; which deal with things completely familiar to them, and which are interesting. (We have seen teachers fall into such a restricted pattern of questioning that almost any question can be answered with one of the following and still gain a nod of approval: "God," "Jesus," "Be good," "Be kind." Don't ever get to be one of those teachers!) Conversation is also stimulated by showing pictures or objects. It is stimulated by a situation in the room to which the teacher calls attention. Conversation is encouraged by other conversation; in fact, one thing leads to another, and it is here that the teacher may need skill because it will not be unusual for one child to dive into the conversational pool and come up a long way off. Without expressing disapproval, and if possible, through using some element of the child's contribution, the teacher must get the group back on the conversational track. This may be done by saying, "Thank you, Ginny. Now let's get back to talking about ways to help Mother. How do you help sometimes, Jack?" Or "Well, Ginny's cat surely can do wonderful tricks. Taking care of our pets is one way we can help at home. Can you think of another, Sue?" Try always to use the children's ideas and to give them a sense of satisfaction in sharing them.

Keep the conversation moving along toward a goal which you have in mind — a group conclusion or an accumulation of experiences which will help to carry out the purposes of the session. Wind it up with a "punch line," *not* a moralizing statement. "You people surely do find a great many ways to help at home. Let's tell God thank you for our homes, and thank you that we can help there!" (Pray briefly.) How much more effective than saying, "Well, God wants all little boys and girls to help at home. So be sure you help Mother all you can."

Most teachers find it helpful to have a great many ways of putting in conversational sparks, and to vary these constantly. It might be helpful to build a list if you are a beginning teacher. These would include such ideas as:

"What do you think about that, Janie?"

"I believe Karen has a suggestion for us."

"Now let's hear from Billy."

"Gerry needs a little time to think. Let's be polite. Now tell us, Gerry, what helper comes to your house?"

"Hank has forgotten what he wanted to say. We all forget sometimes. You just think about it, Hank; we can come back to you."

"That is good thinking, Kathie. Maybe David has something to add." Fortunately you will find many specific suggestions in your curriculum materials. Study these. Skill in guiding conversation will come with practice. Few experiences in the kindergarten are more fun than really good conversation and no thrill equals the one you will feel when the children contribute ideas which show they are growing in the Christian way. It is important to accept every child's contribution, so long as his contribution is serious and his own good thinking. Do not say, "That's right," and stop when the right answer comes, thus cutting off conversation and creative thinking.

## DRAMATIC PLAY

When we examine the behavior of the four-to-six-year-old, we find that dramatic play is characteristic of his social experience. He organizes himself and his friends into a train crew, a zoo, or a family picnic on a moment's notice. His keen imagination enables him to participate realistically in every type of impersonation and he can become a machine, an animal or another person with great ease. His imagination is so fluid that he can transform himself into one thing and then another in rapid succession. Although a costume is not at all essential, it must be admitted that he finds a great deal of satisfaction in the provision of anything which represents a costume. His imagination provides the rest and no elaborate costuming or realistic props are necessary.

With this natural bent to playing a part, it is sound teaching procedure to provide many opportunities for children to engage in dramatic play in the kindergarten. Within a single session this may take various forms. Let us look at each of these and see how we can make use of them as effective ways to help children learn.

**Impersonation.** Opportunity for dramatic play is given in the housekeeping area, for inevitably the child who chooses this corner for play will become a mommy cooking breakfast, a daddy taking care of the baby, a visiting neighbor, a baby, a fixit man, or some other person who might enter a home situation. He seldom, if ever, is himself. If he remains a child at all, he is usually somebody else. In the block corner he may use stand-up figures for dramatic play or he may make a building with larger blocks and, going inside of it, become a storekeeper, a fireman, an organist, or any other grownup whose activities appeal to him.

Opportunities for less dramatic impersonation occur in various forms during games, in which, for example, he might be a postman delivering a letter. Children might also act out a situation as part of a larger group activity, such as singing as they pretend to be going to church as families.

**Action Songs or Poems.** Many songs we use in kindergarten offer opportunities for bits of dramatic play. Fingers may become leaves fluttering down or arms clock pendulums accompanying the words and music of a song with appropriate action. This serves the double purpose of adding to the children's interest through employing the dramatic play technique, and of providing the physical action which is necessary for ongoing interest. The four-to-six-year-old cannot long remain in an inactive position and continue to give attention. Motion is almost as essential to him as breathing!

An action poem will serve the same purpose. It, too, will give opportunity for everyone to participate simultaneously in some physical effort and still keep the group attention running along in a single interest. It offers a very agreeable change of pace.

In the case of both the action song and the action poem, the teacher does not need to give instructions to the children about what to do. She may merely suggest, "Here is a song (or poem) we can do together about ——." As she uses the song or poem she is seated where the group can see, and they copy the actions with which she accompanies the words. Many times these actions require the use of the fingers and hands only, and may not be thought of as dramatic experiences in the usual sense. However, they are dramatic in that the child is acting out or interpreting with his hands.

It is important for you, the teacher, to know these action songs and poems so well that it will be unnecessary to stop and read, or to figure out what comes next. You will need to practice them ahead of time.

All such action songs or poems should be correlated with the session purpose and not used merely to fill time. They can be used in transition periods (guiding the group from one activity to another) but even then, it is better if they are related to the session. Rightly used, they can be an asset to teaching; an aid to achieving the purpose of the session.

**Playing a Story.** The validity of acting out a story is readily recognized when we remember that children retain in their minds the things they *do* longer and more accurately than they retain what they *hear,* or even what they hear *and see.* Add to this the natural readiness of the kindergarten child to enter into dramatic play of any kind, and it becomes immediately obvious that in playing a story, we have an excellent way of helping children to learn.

Steps in using this activity with kindergarten children may be outlined as follows:

1. Tell the story, preferably using a picture.

2. Have children suggest the characters needed. "If we were going to play this story, what people would we need?" They may start in immediately to say, "I want to be the ——," but it is wise to do the choosing of the players later, after your list of characters is made up, since this gives you more time to size up the situation. This helps you not to make the mistake of choosing reluctant players who pour cold water on the enthusiasm by saying "I don't want to!" and to avoid the equally undesirable pitfall of ending up with all the most aggressive people in the parts.

3. Locate the set. "What places were in this story?" "Where shall we have the ....?" Children will suggest, "The field could be over by the book table." They may suggest a few props: "Let's play this red book is the fire."

4. Choose the characters, and give each his starting place. "Pat may be Mary. Now we need some shepherds to go out in the field to watch their sheep. The field is over by the book table and the angels are going to hide in the house corner." Jot down characters as you choose them so you will be sure to give turns to other children in the future.

5. Begin the action. To help children enjoy their experience, be sure of themselves, and to keep action moving smoothly, it is a good idea to tell the story as action proceeds, suggesting the action pointedly in the telling. Children will readily follow such cues as, "Now the shepherds are walking out to the field, step, step, step. They sit down where they can see all the sheep." They will not be likely to contribute many speaking parts until the story has been played enough times for them to feel familiar with it. It only cramps their freedom to tell them what to say, but you may suggest speaking parts by saying, "Now the angel is telling the shepherds not to be afraid. What has he come to tell them?"

Sometimes by taking a part herself the teacher can step out of her role as teacher and, telling the story from a player's viewpoint, keep the action moving. Find examples of playing Bible stories in your curriculum materials and note how the procedures move.

6. Evaluate. "How could we play the story better?" Evaluation should be done mostly by the children. Suggestions will relate to the way actors played. Costumes or props might be added. Commend the performers.

7. Play the story again. Children will gain increasing pleasure with a repetition. In a later session, the play may be done again.

**Rhythm Sequences or Rhythmic Play.** In this form of dramatic play, an action is suggested to be carried out rhythmically with a musical accompaniment on the piano or record player. When the actions are threaded together with a few words, we have a *rhythm sequence* or *rhythmic play*. If, for example, the teacher suggests, "We'll play some things we do on a snowy day," and follows this with a series of activities, each with its own suitable music, this may be thought of as a *rhythm sequence*. In this case the activities might be as follows: Putting on outdoor clothes and boots, walking in deep snow, shoveling a path, making a snowball and rolling it in the snow to make it bigger; making a snowman, and throwing snowballs at it; being snowflakes as it begins to snow again, then running into the house and taking off outside clothes. All of this is "pretend," but with a brief bit of music to add to the children's vivid imagination, it can be very real.

In choosing the music, select something from a half minute to a minute long with a quality which matches the suggested action and a rhythm (2/4, 4/4, or 3/4) best suited to the motion which is to be done. In playing it use the tempo and volume which fit the activity, and accent the first beat of the measure slightly to make the rhythm more obvious. In church kindergarten the important thing is not the rhythmic response; the important thing rather is to let the music add to the realism of the dramatic play. The activities must again be correlated with the theme of the session if their presence in the curriculum is to be of value in achieving our purposes. There is no place for rhythmic activity just to fill in time in the Sunday session.

## STORYTIME

Jesus was fully aware of the power of the story in teaching. His stories always were related to the point he was trying to make. They were concise but with enough vivid detail to stir the imagination. They came close to the experience of the listeners. They were full of action. These qualities should be characteristic of the story told in the kindergarten as well. Because of the ages of our listeners we must add other criteria: the story must be simple in vocabulary and have no involved sentence structure. It will be more effective if it contains words that imitate natural sounds, much direct discourse, and elements of repetition.

Curriculum materials are rich in stories so that the responsibility for selection is made very easy for the teacher. It is good to be aware, however, of qualities which make up a good story.

In your choice of picture-story books, in addition to knowing the qualities of a good story, stated above, you will need to choose books with bright, simple, artistically good pictures. There should be only a few lines of print on each page. The overall length of the story is important, for no story is good enough to hold the attention of a group of kindergarteners if it is too long. It is better to select a short story and be besieged by the request, "Read it again!" than to plow on through the last pages of a book with waning attention and general boredom. You will learn quickly about how long your group will remain enchanted by the magic of a story. The span of attention varies from group to group depending on the age of the children and depending on the combinations of personalities which make up the group. Of course, the magic of the story itself helps to determine the attention span.

What is your most effective means of presenting a story to a group?

1. *Have the group ready for a story before you begin.* This means they will have recently had some physical activity so they are able to enjoy sitting. It means the group will all be seated where they can see your face (and the pages of the picture book, if you are using one) without moving around. It means you will have the attention of everyone before you begin to tell the story, and that they are ready to hear the story. Sometimes you will want to give an introductory statement but it should never "give away" the main idea of the story. You might say, "It's storytime now. Today we have a story about something Jesus did," but not, "I am going to tell you a story about how Jesus made a sick man well."

2. *Tell the story well!* This means you will know the story, and you will be able to use expression which adds to the children's enjoyment. In general, your voice will be relaxed and pleasant with a fairly low pitch. When the story becomes exciting, you may speed up your rate and raise the pitch just a little for two or three sentences. If the story calls for the sound of raindrops your voice will softly and rhythmically clip off "pit-pat, pit-pat, pit-pat, pit-pat," or if a cat walks into the story you will be able to make his plaintive "meow" sound like a real cat, because you have practiced meowing until you can make that cat meow in a real way.

You will not hurry your story, but you will not drag it either. Give the children time to enjoy the full flavor as you move along at a deliberate pace, enjoying it yourself.

Remember that anyone who is willing to take the time to

do so can become a good storyteller. Be careful to use the words and ideas which the writer has used and do not change the meaning of the story. Some storytellers fail because they do not *know* the story well enough to tell it. When they do not know the story, they tend to use words which the children do not understand. A good story can be ruined in the telling of it!

A few stories are so well written that they must be *read* to do them justice. When this is the case, remember to be familiar with the story so that you can read it easily, looking at the children as much as possible.

When you read from a picture book, face the children and hold the book open wide and perfectly vertical, in one hand. Turn your body slightly so you can look at the words without getting your head in the way of the children's view. Practice turning the pages without lowering the book or changing the angle. Hold the book at least a foot away from your face. Before you begin, be sure every child is seated on a rug or in a chair so that he can see the pages clearly.

Never interrupt your story by saying "I forgot," or by injecting yourself into the picture with an opinion. And do not interrupt it by a question which will break the thread of the story by beginning a discussion. Certain questions might have a place, as after the sentence, "George was very curious," you might ask, "What is 'curious'?" and after a child or two has had a chance to explain, go right back to the story saying, "Yes, George was curious. George wanted to find out."

Do not interrupt your story by recognizing irrelevant interruptions. Simply ignore them, weave them into the story, or handle them very briefly, "It's the story's turn to talk, Ann," and go right on. To do more loses the thread of the story and the attention of the entire group.

Watch the skilled storyteller and analyze her success; practice and find your own style and manner of most effective storytelling. The story is being told well when every child is sitting with his attention captivated and when the end of a story brings responses which say, "We loved it!"

Finally, be ready to tell the story at any time during the session. Perhaps, in an interest center, you will find *one* child ready for the story; tell it then.

## CREATIVE ACTIVITIES

Cutting, coloring, pasting, and making things is so much a part of the kindergarten that it is hard to visualize a kindergarten in which these things would not go on with a great deal of learning and fun for the children. But these activities are not ends in themselves and when the production of a certain piece of work becomes a purpose rather than a means to an end, it frankly has no place in any well-run kindergarten.

This does not mean that we will not plan for such activities; it means only that we will set them in their proper perspective. What place then do these activities have as a teaching method, and how shall we make them best serve the children's needs?

We will deal with the last part of this question first, considering ways of making activities contribute most to children's needs.

(a) *Let the activity always be something children can do* at their own pace and in their own way. Too small cutting or coloring, or too complicated assembly will end up being frustrating or being done by the teacher. The four-to-six-year-old has limited skill in the use of his small muscles.

(b) *Show an example of the finished work* to help children know how to proceed.

(c) *Make directions clear, specific, and concise.* Accompany them with demonstration.

(d) *Encourage children to work out their own ideas.* Stress every child's work being done in his own way. To quote from the "Children's Leader" section of the *Baptist Leader* (July, 1955, page 25):

"The teacher . . . will want to give children a feeling of freedom about doing activities in their own way. Frequently children with their endless ingenuity will discover ways to carry out an activity which will really be better than the ways the leader has planned. Results from a given piece of work should never bear the stereotyped resemblance of being 'all alike,' but each finished piece of work should have the stamp of the child's individuality upon it. It is the attitude of the leader which determines the 'climate' in which a child will feel free to work out his own ideas, confident that they will be accepted and appreciated.

"A five-year-old, being picked up at the door of the kindergarten, greeted his mother with a dejected air. His mother looked at the piece of paper he held in his hand. On it he had drawn a gay orange tree—all orange, and blowing in the wind.

" 'What a nice tree!' she commented brightly.

"He shook his head. 'I should have made it green,' he said. 'The teacher said it should have been green.'

"Mother usually upheld 'teacher' but she said honestly, 'I think it is a rather beautiful tree. I *like* it *orange!*'

" 'So do I,' Kevin admitted. 'But we all have to make trees green in my kindergarten.'

"When a teacher stifles initiative and insists on her own ideas being carried out in a dictatorial fashion, children do not learn to think for themselves and they do not feel adequate, free, or satisfied with the results of what they make and do."

(e) *Give the child occasional suggestions in the technique of handling materials.* "Suppose you try putting the paste on in a smaller lump, then push it around smooth with no 'lumpy-bumpies' " will usually bring an appreciative response. Or, "Maybe you'd find it easier to hold the scissors like this. It's such hard work the way you're doing it," will give the child a new impetus for finishing a job.

(f) *Encourage the child to do his best and to finish his work* by such comments as the following:

"You have done a good job. You still have a space over here. What could you crayon here to make your picture even more interesting?"

"Take your time, Billy. You are working a little too fast. There's no need to hurry."

"I like the colors you have used. Tell me about your picture."

"That is nice cutting. You are almost finished. Just take off this little 'squiggle' here and you'll be ready to paste, don't you think?"

What feelings do these comments convey to the child? What response will he be likely to make?

(g) *Put his name on his work while he is working* and you will avoid many problems.

(h) *Be sure he has a place for finished work,* enjoys cleaning up his work space, and remembers to take home finished work which is his. Have a place for unfinished work so it can be finished in the next session.

Having examined the ways of guiding activities, let us consider the ways in which creative activities may contribute to accomplishing our purposes in kindergarten. Working with crayons, paper, scissors, paste, and other materials gives children an opportunity to express the ideas they have gained. For example, the mural on which children work together, drawing the crowd of people with Zacchaeus up in the tree trying to see over their heads, recalls the story from a previous Sunday. It also deepens the impression they received from hearing the story.

Through making something, children may have a share in some service project which puts friendliness into action. This would be the case when get-well cards are made for the minister to deliver in making calls, or when invitations are made to invite new people in the neighborhood to church.

Making things may stimulate children's interest in some subject, inviting them to discover facts for themselves. Turning a box into a Palestinian house calls for looking at pictures to discover "what kind of house the woman of Shunem and her husband lived in, and how they could put a room on the roof. What kind of roof was it?"

Character traits, like working out problems co-operatively, gaining self-confidence through the satisfaction of achieving some creative work, learning to take responsibility, doing one's part for the good of all and sharing materials with others may be developed through experiences of making things in the kindergarten. All traits become stronger as they are practiced, and there is opportunity to practice each of these over and over as children work together to make things.

This summary of some of the values in giving opportunity for making things is by no means exhaustive, but will serve to show that this teaching method has a justifiable place in the kindergarten.

## EXPERIENCES IN WORSHIP

Church kindergarten should be an experience not only of talking about God and thinking of him but one of sensing his presence and of talking with him. This is worship, to recognize the presence of God and to communicate with him. Worship experiences stand in a unique place in the kindergarten morning, for they are both the embodiment of one of our teaching objectives, and a means to the end of achieving our purposes. They provide moments of insight in which the child's fellowship with God grows. Such moments of worship may furnish such satisfaction in a sense of knowing God that the child will be led to know God better and to want to live in accordance with his plan.

Enigmatically, though these worship experiences occupy a place of crucial importance in the kindergarten, it is difficult for curriculum writers to offer you definite plans for them. Suggestions can be made as to how the worship experiences may occur, but they may never happen exactly that way. Perhaps this is because God himself enters so really into the picture, making his presence felt at an unexpected moment; this is the moment to seize for a real worship experience. This idea is a very exciting one, is it not? It places upon you, the teacher, the responsibility of recognizing the moment at which the child or children may reach out and touch God's hand because there he is in the midst of you!

Children have some times of genuine meditation and thinking things through but it is asking too much to expect them all to put themselves in a frame of mind for five minutes of worship from ten o'clock to five after ten every Sunday morning. They simply cannot discipline themselves to think abstractly. They cannot open their minds to God at will as a grownup should be able to do. Therefore, the teacher tries to bring them experiences which may create the opportunity to feel that God is near; to be quiet and to talk with him. In her own sensitivity to their needs and reactions, and in her own sensitivity to God, the teacher becomes aware that God is near and opens the door to worship. This can happen at any time in the morning. Just as you have your times set aside for worship in your everyday living and still become aware of God at an unexpected moment — while you are walking to the bus line, watching a sunset, pouring a glass of milk for a hungry child, talking with a friend — so he may confront a group at an unpredictable moment. God is there all the time, it is simply a matter of our spirits being tuned to an awareness of his presence.

When are these moments likely to occur in the kindergarten? Are there any signposts that may alert the teacher to "Be ready, now!"? Analysis has shown that *children will often be ready to worship at the following times:*

1. *When they are enjoying something beautiful from God's world.* This may be out-of-doors or it may be something they are watching from a window, but perhaps most frequently it is something which has been brought into the room.

2. *When they are aware of fellowship with other children or adults.* This might be at a time when a church helper or special visitor has been invited to the group and they have been led to think about this person. It might be a time of realizing the love of parents or the fun of having playmates, or the needs of people who are ill or have not heard of God's love. It might come at a time when the group is visiting a shut-in or the minister in his study or the organist in the sanctuary.

3. *When they are having a moment of high emotional experience.* This is difficult to pin down and describe. You may be able to tell by the expression on their faces, or by the revealing comment of some child. Frequently this comes when children are thinking about Jesus and his kindliness. Perhaps there is a second of silence and Ruth says, "Jesus was *always* helping somebody, wasn't he?" The teacher grasps this moment, noting the readiness of the group, and says, "Let's talk with God about Jesus. (Pause.) We thank you, O God, for Jesus who was always helping somebody. We are glad he was so loving and kind, always loving people as you do. Amen."

The "high emotional experience" will be a moment of love, awe, and devotion inseparably intermingled. It may also come at the end of a story or conversation.

4. *When they are working on or have completed some work of service to others.* A sense of gladness for a share in helping pack a basket of fruit for a grandmother with a broken

hip; a feeling of joy as we put into the box the last mittens from our mitten tree for boys and girls with cold fingers; a wave of happiness as we think about the money gifts we have just brought for friends in Mexico who are going to hear Bible stories because we shared; these are the kinds of things which may "spark" the fire of worship.

What does the teacher do when she senses the moment for worship? She may say, "Let us talk with God about it," or "Let us tell God how we feel about ——," or "Let's say thank you to God," pause a second or two, then in simple words of two or three sentences at the most express the appropriate thought to God. This might be followed by a song or a Bible verse introduced by saying, "We could sing about God's leaves" and "Our Bible has something to say about God's beautiful world" (or about whatever appropriately introduces the song or verse). Sometimes the song or the Bible verse will come first, and then the prayer.

Prayer always should be addressed to God. While "We thank thee" is simple and reverent enough to be suitable for kindergarten, other second person references should be "you," not "thee" and "thou," and some teachers prefer to carry the less formal "you" into all conversation with God. Brevity is a necessity if the whole group is to be kept in the spirit of worship; three sentences is the maximum, and all of these sentences should be simple ones. There may be several worship moments in one session. It will not always be an experience of the whole group; it may be there are only a few children or just one with whom the teacher is working when she senses the opportunity for worship. She does not wait for hands to be folded and eyes closed and lose the moment thereby in the mechanics of prayer. She assumes a reverent posture herself with eyes closed and head bowed, and using a tone of voice neither weighty with formality nor casual with informality, brings children the keen awareness of God.

In prayer particularly we need to guard against the generalizations which lack meaning for children. "Help us to be kind," "be good," or "to share" may be just words with no meaning, while "Help us to remember to put away our toys," or "come when Mother calls," or "let other children have turns with our bikes and wagons," may have significant effects upon action. Four-to-six-year-olds are beginning to form general concepts of "kindness" and "goodness" so that they can go from the specific situation to the general. They begin to know that helping a child who falls to get back on his feet is a form of kindness. But they have great difficulty going from the general to the particular and the use of a term like "kindness" is of practically no value — in prayer or in conversation either.

Perhaps a word should be said about the form prayer. This does have an occasional place in the kindergarten, particularly as a grace. However, there is a danger in using one over several Sundays or even in building up a repertoire of little rhyming prayers which are used interchangeably week after week. Very little thought is necessary when these prayers are used, and it will be easy for children to fall into the habit of repeating words routinely, thinking this is prayer. It is better to vary the prayer, giving it content which is significant for the particular occasion at hand. Sometimes suitable variables can be inserted in the form prayer, giving it special meaning as it applies to the situation, or sometimes the pattern of a prayer may be followed using a change in wording. The chant, "Thanks for juice, thanks for juice; thanks for cookies too," may be changed to apply to the food to be eaten on a different occasion, "Thanks for milk, thanks for milk; thanks for crackers too." If form prayers are used, then guard zealously against any routine and "vain repetition."

As the teacher prepares for a session she will need to have several possible resources ready for use when the opportunity for worship arrives. Knowing the theme of the session, she will have ready in her mind (and perhaps jotted down on a card to impress them on her mind, *not* for reference)

a Bible verse or two or three,

several songs from which she may choose and which express thanks to or thoughts of God,

possible prayer sentences,

an offering dedication,

an occasional poem,

conversation ideas with reference to God's nearness.

There often will come the awareness that the group is in the very presence of God. The teacher has privilege of leading children into that wonderful awareness!

## REST AND RELAXATION

We live in the age of coffee breaks and pauses that refresh, of advice to take a change of pace and go back with renewed enthusiasm to what we have been doing. Scientific studies show that we work better and learn better if we take time out for something different and then return to our main effort. This has not always been recognized at the adult level, but teachers of young children have noticed for many years that the last part of a two-hour session went much more successfully when children had a few minutes to enjoy a small cup of milk or juice and a cracker, then to stretch out full length and relax. Undeniably living in a group is more stimulating and demanding than going one's separate way, and when children become tired they are more difficult to guide and they do not gain as much from group living or from any activity.

In addition to these facts, the inclusion of a "snack" of fruit or juice and cracker gives an opportunity to teach the habit of saying grace before meals. In many cases teachers have discovered that families have found it necessary to begin to pray before their meals at home simply because the children attending kindergarten showed them the way.

Relaxation time is usually included as such only in the longer session, but there should be elements of relaxation in the shorter session as well. Through the use of this term "relaxation time" we should not lose sight of the fact that the good kindergarten is *constantly* relaxed in feeling and tone. There is an ease and deliberateness, a freedom from hurry, that is characteristic of the attitude of all the teachers.

If the toileting facilities are not adjacent to the room, a teacher will need to take the children in small groups to give them the help and supervision they need. Even though the washroom is directly off the kindergarten, time and effort will be saved, when several children are toileting and washing up, if one teacher gives her full attention to the children using these facilities. Some children love the feel of soapsuds, and within reason, the teacher should not hurry them along. She may even take the opportunity to say something to this effect, "Aren't you glad God planned for us to have water for washing? Look at the colors shining in the tiny soap bubbles. Washing is such fun." Or, "You are washing your hands nice and clean. It's always good to do a good job of such things!"

Back in the room some children (who had the first turn to wash so they could carry out assigned responsibilities) are placing napkins, a cup of juice, and a cracker at each place. Some teachers keep small plastic aprons on hand for these lunch helpers as extra insurance against spills on Sunday-best clothes.

Other children in the room are enjoying books, a record or an easy game while waiting for their turn to get ready for juice, or while waiting for juice to be ready. The teacher will need to see that everyone is happily busy with something he enjoys at this time, but toys and materials are not to be gotten out for this would require another cleaning-up job.

When juice is ready and everyone is washed, children may find places. If your kindergarten is grouped in families, the leading teacher will call a family at a time; if you have a large group, she may call all the children with black shoes, or all the children with red on, or all the children with stripes on their clothes first, following the first group with calling other similar categories. This makes a game of going to the tables and saves a sudden rush.

It avoids spills to have children stand behind chairs till grace is said or to have them sit with hands in laps, singing perhaps to a sing-song tune:

"Hands in laps, hands in laps, everybody ready with hands in laps."

After grace, when the food has been eaten, children should be encouraged to stay at the table and not walk around the room, just talking to their friends until the people at the table have all finished and the leading teacher calls them, a table at a time, to get ready for rest. A child may pass the waste basket around each table to receive cups and napkins or each child may throw away his cup and napkin as he gets up from the table and pushes in his chair.

Children should be allowed to talk while they are getting ready to rest; the teacher may have to help them get their mats in rows so that heads and feet are alternated. When everyone or almost everyone is down, she may say, "No more voices now; it's all-quiet time." Sometimes she will want to make a game of getting ready for rest, pretending to be the mother "tucking her children in" and pantomiming this activity, or suggesting children pretend they are boys and girls of Jesus' time, unrolling their mats and lying down on the flat roof where they can see the stars. This play can be correlated often with the theme of the session.

After at least ten minutes of quiet, the leading teacher may sing, use recordings with a pleasant quiet quality, or read poetry or tell a story. Though a story is not usually recommended, it might be all right to read a story brought in by a child or tell a story with a repetitious musical quality. Rest on the mats should last about fifteen minutes.

Do not call all the children at once when it is time to get up, or grand confusion will result. Instead call them individually, "Jane, you may put away your mat and sit near the piano. Scott, you were a good rester, you may put away your mat and sit near the piano."

Relaxation time often includes some special musical activity, either using large motions or rhythm instruments. Sometimes it includes a musical game or a game without music. It is very important for it to include some physical activity using large muscles, for children find this very restful too if the tone is kept deliberate.

## VISITS AND RESOURCE PERSONS

Grownups other than the teachers and regular staff members may have much to contribute to the church school session. Consulting your enrollment cards you will find parents whose hobbies and occupations can be used to enrich the children's experience when they relate to the purposes of the session. Other adults in the church who serve the church or the community in special ways also may have a place as guests in the kindergarten room, as may grownups or children from another country or culture.

Such visits always are planned with a purpose and with the idea of choosing a person who will know how to mingle interestingly with young children and will appeal to them.

Guests are consulted in advance and it is explained to them what children are learning and how they may be most helpful. However, an alert teacher will not overlook the possibility of the unexpected presence of the pastor in the room on a Sunday morning and will utilize his visit even though it was not planned ahead.

To start your thinking we suggest here a few possibilities for visitors:

| Session Idea | Visitor |
|---|---|
| Grown-up friends work in our church. | The pastor, caretaker, a trustee, usher, choir member, treasurer |
| People in our community help us. | A postman, policeman, doctor, nurse, milkman (in uniform) |
| People of other countries are friends of ours. | A Latin American, Oriental, European (in native costume) or someone who has visited there |
| God has given us ears to enjoy beautiful sounds. | An instrumentalist or singer |
| Families are fun. | A grandmother or a baby |
| People work with God in his beautiful world. | A farmer, gardener, forester, nurseryman |

This list will only begin to make you aware of the many possibilities. When children have written a letter of invitation (dictated it) and planned for a visitor to tell them about something they want to know, they will anticipate the visit with relish. They will gain not only the knowledge which the visitor shares, but they will gain a sense of the wider fellowship of the church which reaches beyond their own room. They will have opportunity to practice Christian hospitality as they learn to provide for the comfort of their guest, and they will learn the graciousness of appreciation as they express their thanks for the service.

Another enrichment feature for the kindergarten program is to plan visits for the children to see something or someone, or to hear something which will enrich their learning for a particular session. This might be a visit to the church grounds to see outdoor beauty, or a visit to another part of the church to see how that area of the church is used, or to see a church worker busy there. It might be a carefully planned visit to a nearby shut-in or to see a lovely garden. Any such visit should be purposeful, and planned with care.

If children are to be taken away from the church, which would probably be a rare thing, parents should know ahead of time, and a note of permission be granted by each. Some teachers like to use a long smooth rope with a loop at the front to be held by the leading teacher, while the children and helping teachers walk on each side of the rope, holding it. Sometimes a few parents may be invited ahead of time to go along as extra helpers.

The values of a visit should be gathered up in a discussion when the children return to the kindergarten room, and they should be given opportunities for drawing pictures about their experience and for dictating a story about what happened. Each child can contribute a sentence to a story; if your group is large, stories should be written in groups of ten or twelve. Sometimes the "stories" can be duplicated so each child may have a copy. He may then draw pictures to illustrate the story. At other times the "story" might be offered as copy for the church paper.

## CREATIVITY WITH WORDS

Children can work with materials to express their ideas—we all know that. But some of us make far less use of their ability to create with words than we might. This should be utilized in the kindergarten. One way of doing so is in the way just mentioned above. Children may also create group stories about other group experiences — projects in service, a unit they specially enjoy, or a co-operative venture in making something, such as a large cardboard packing-case church, in which they dramatize the work of church helpers and play going to church.

The technique to be employed in "writing" this group story is as follows:

1. Gather a group of eight or ten children on a rug on the floor in front of you.

2. Have in your hands a pencil and a sheet of white paper clipped to a board to make it easy to write. Seat yourself in front of the group.

3. Announce your purpose and procedure: "We have finished a fine big church today. Let's make a story about it. Everybody will have a turn to tell something. Todd, would

you start us off and tell us how we began our church? Or tell us something you like about it?"

4. Write quickly each child's contribution *as he gives it,* except for changing "I" to the child's name. Instead of writing "I helped paint the walls with red bricks," write "Dick helped paint the walls with red bricks."

5. Give each child a turn, encouraging the less outgoing ones with some question or comment. "What do you want to tell about our church, Carol?" (Pause.) "No one has told how we play in it. Maybe you would tell about that. How *do* we play in it?"

6. Read the finished story back to the group and then ask "is there anything we left out? Do you have anything to add?"

7. Have it duplicated for the following session or print it in large letters on a sheet of paper for the wall. Skilled teachers may use these techniques to help children work together to write not only original stories, but also poems or plays. Letters, too, may be dictated by the group, inviting guests or thanking them. Letters to the parents may be dictated when the group has decided that a special message should go home. These would need to be duplicated.

There are many other uses for children's creative ability with words in the kindergarten. After a mural has been painted each child may tell about his work. The "legend" going from left to right may be carefully printed with one sentence under another, then posted under or near the mural on the wall.

A child may tell the teacher the "story" of the crayon or paint picture he has made. The teacher may print this sentence or two neatly across the top of the picture if there is unused space there, or the words may be printed on a separate strip of paper to be pasted or mounted beneath the picture.

Greeting cards made by the children have much more charm and a more personal touch if they dictate the message for the teacher to write inside. This takes time, of course, and the teacher will need to begin going around to children as soon as they start to work, write the message for one at a time, then let him continue work. Do not be surprised when some will not have a message to dictate.

Sometimes a story or poem which the children have written may be printed and mounted along with a drawing or cut-and-paste illustration, in a place where all the parents and church friends can enjoy it. Children find much satisfaction in writing the stories, in hearing them, and in having them put to use. They feel about them as they do about their art work — proud and pleased. Let's put to work this method of translating experiences into their own words, and we as well as they will be delighted with their charming and vivid way of putting things. Their story contributions may also serve as a check on what they have been learning.

## CREATIVE MUSIC

Just as we have been slow to recognize the child's potential to create with words and to give it a place in the program, so their capacity for creating songs has been utilized by only a very few teachers.

The young child makes up songs of his own while he is at work or play. These come spontaneously and are simply his own thoughts set to music with no regard to the adult rules of song-making. They possess a rhythm which may or may not bear resemblance to the patterns familiar to adults. Tunes range from random note sequences to rather well-balanced melodies. Sometimes the songs go on and on telling a story that seems to have no end; sometimes songs are short and may or may not make a bit of sense to the grownup. Occasionally a child with a special facility for rhyme or rhythm will spontaneously come forth with a song which has both a traditional measure pattern and rhymes in a pattern as well. This is the exception, however, and not characteristic of the usual spontaneous song of the four-to-six-year-old.

To what use can we put this facility for song-making; this natural manner in which the young child expresses his ideas; this joy that overflows at random in spontaneous singing?

Children can make up their own tunes to Bible verses. "Let's give this Bible verse a tune. Many parts of our Bible are sung by choirs. Many parts have been made into hymns that our mommies and daddies sing in church. We can sing things that are in the Bible too. All we need to do is give our verse a tune. Who would like to have the first turn to sing it?" When the experience is new and the teacher meets with hesitancy, it will be due to the children's uncertainty, not their inability. Probably five or six children will clamor for turns. You may call on each child, commend him, then go on to the next. If no one volunteers, you may need to show them what you mean, as we need to do in so many other kindergarten procedures. Say, "You could sing it this way," and sing the verse once, "or this way," and sing it a different way, "or this way," and sing it a third way. Then say, "Now we are ready for your tunes. How would you sing it, Ann Lee?"

Should one tune be particularly catchy or fitting, the whole group may learn it. Be sure to get it down so that it can be sung again in the same way in the next session. Many children's songs are based on the pattern 1,1,2,1 as, "The Farmer in the Dell" in which lines are all alike in words except for the third line; or on the pattern, 1,1,1,2 as "Mulberry Bush" in which the first three lines are alike and the last one different. Children may follow the first pattern if a more elaborate song is to be created.

Words might be:

    Do good, and share what you have, (1)
    Do good, and share what you have, (1)
    Look around and find ways to help, (2)
    Do good, and share what you have. (1)

Or, for the other pattern the words might be:

    The flowers appear on the earth; (1)
    The flowers appear on the earth; (1)
    The flowers appear on the earth, (1)
    And the time of the singing of birds is come. (2)

Carrying out these ideas will give your group a good start in song-making. Then you can go on to songs with original words simply by asking, after a conversation about fun at home, a walk outdoors, a discussion about God's care or a picture about Jesus, "Who has a song about it? What could we say about it? What can we sing?"

The next step will be that any time at all you may expect a child to come to you and say, "I have a song!" Of course, you stop immediately and listen because songs have a habit of getting away from us. This is the chief problem any of us have met as we use this teaching method. We wish we were more adept at getting down words and music fast enough to save every song that is created! It is comforting to know, however, that even if the song does get away, the act of creating it has done something for the Christian growth of the singer, and, if it has been shared with the whole group, it may have contributed to the Christian growth of all of the children.

It is necessary to add that not every teacher has the musical ability to write down music as suggested in the foregoing paragraphs. Do *not* allow this to dampen the musical creativity of the children, however. Let them create songs even if they cannot be preserved but, if at all possible, make sure that one of your teachers has this needed musical ability.

## GAMES

Games have a place in the church kindergarten when they are chosen with a purpose and used in a spirit of easy, pleasant participation. Not all children's games have a place for, as in everything else, we measure value by what the activity has to contribute to the purpose of the session and the readiness of the children to participate. Kindergarten children are ready only for small group games and simple rhythms.

In the foregoing paragraphs we have explained some ways to help kindergarten children to learn. Putting them into practice, you will begin to develop your own techniques of handling them. Please note that there is no *one* way of doing things! Experience will show you how to improve your skills; observing other teachers will add new insights; and reading will open new possibilities to you. Your techniques should improve from year to year, and your approach to a situation remain fresh and challenging. Becoming a *good* teacher is an ongoing, endless process. You have made a good start! Resolve here and now that you will neither jump from one thing to another nor settle down into a rut. Rather, be determined to practice the things you know best and to do them in the best way. Try the new technique after thorough preparation and be ever growing, growing, GROWING!

> Our Father, we are learning about the ways children grow. We want to be growing too. Help us not to be overwhelmed by the many teaching skills which we need to develop, but rather, help us to be thrilled that through so many avenues we can make thee known to children. Give us patience with ourselves, but help us not to be contented until we do the best thing in the best way, knowing that only the best is worthy of our high and holy calling to thy service. We pray in Jesus' name. Amen.

## Projects and Discussion Questions

1. Describe one particular interest center. Discuss the teacher's responsibility in preparing this and guiding activities there. Or, prepare an interest center for actual use in the kindergarten and report on children's experiences there under your guidance.
2. Observe a teacher with a kindergarten group and discuss the following: (a) How was the group seated? (b) How was conversation initiated? (c) List verbatim some contributions by the children. (d) List verbatim some questions by the teacher. (e) How did the teacher treat an apparently irrelevant contribution? (f) How did the teacher stimulate children's ideas? (g) What do you think children gained from this conversational experience?
3. Prepare and tell a story, keeping in mind the points on pages 65-67.
4. Discuss the teacher's role in guiding creative activities.
5. Discuss and analyze a worship experience in the kindergarten. In what ways was the teacher prepared ahead of time for the moment of worship? How did the teacher create an atmosphere or readiness for worship? What indications were apparent that the children really felt God's presence?

CHAPTER 5

# OBTAINING A GOOD GROUP RESPONSE

Teachers who are new at leading a kindergarten group have frequently had considerable experience with one or two children of this age. They enjoy the personalities and age characteristics they see displayed by the four-to-six-year-old and recall the fun they have often had with children of this age. It is essential to like children of this age if you are to teach them successfully. You will find that working with a group is quite a different proposition from guiding one or two children. Special techniques are needed to get a good response from a group. While each individual is important and needs to be considered, something more is needed when you are dealing with a group. Although it is the "plus" techniques of guiding a group with which we will attempt to deal here, keep in mind that many activities in the kindergarten are done on an individual basis.

1. *Know what you are doing.* This statement sounds almost too naïve; almost too obvious to include. But it is a very good beginning point for getting a good group response. When teachers are a little foggy in their own minds about what they are doing, children become confused, and the group becomes disorganized. Thorough preparation is a necessity for which no other stroke of ingenuity or wealth of experience can compensate. Be sure you have tried out things you are going to do with the children. Nothing is more disconcerting than to have the teacher try to demonstrate something, and not know how it goes! Most teachers will try this every once in a while, to their sorrow; don't!

If you have to grope for your "notes" to know what to do next and to hold your morning together; if you have to read the action poems; if you have to figure out how the cornucopia is to be made; it's the sad truth — you do not know what you are doing, and children will not know either. To use a few notes is reasonable, but put them on a card in a convenient pocket where you can reach them on a split-second impulse! Visualize your transitions. Know where you are going.

2. *The way you say a thing is important.* A sergeant once grew hopeless about the response he was getting from a new batch of rookies and finally in desperation cried, "Just come out here and look at yourselves!" If we could just *hear* ourselves sometimes we would be able to tell immediately why we are not getting a better response from a group. Tone of voice is a key to group response, and so is pitch. Men teachers have a natural advantage at this point. Pitch your voice low but give it sufficient volume to be heard by every child in the room. Do not speak in a monotone nor with rapid variation in tone. Make your diction clear; give directions concisely and positively. Let your tone express friendliness without being artificial. And, assume co-operation without being overbearing. Be deliberate about what you say so that children will be certain to understand it. Use vocabulary that leaves no guesswork on the children's part as to what you mean. Do not allow yourself to stumble into the pitfalls of using, "Sh-h-h-h-h!" or "Children, now be quiet," or "Didn't you hear me?" These and many similar expressions are a waste of breath! Use good psychology and good common sense in the way you express yourself.

Here are some examples of how to say things the right way. Examine them, and see if they are an improvement over the way you say it.

1. "I'm sure you can do this. You are a fine four-year-old and that means you can do it nicely," instead of "Be a big boy now," or "Don't be a baby."
2. "The clock says it's time to _____," instead of "Do this for me now," or, "I want you to _____."
3. "You are not to (hit) in kindergarten. It hurts and it

makes us all unhappy," instead of "Stop (hitting). That's naughty."

4. "I'll help you as soon as I've finished helping Susan," instead of "Just wait a minute."
5. "It's not your turn to talk now, Stephen," instead of, "Be quiet, Stephen."
6. "If you had listened, John, you would have known. Please listen next time," instead "Why didn't you listen?"
7. "You can work more carefully, Steve. Please try," instead of "You are careless (or noisy, or any other negative)."
8. "You are using outside voices. No one can hear you when you yell inside. Please speak so we can hear you," instead of "Sh-h-h-h-h!"
9. "We have a rule against running in the room. It's not safe," instead of "You're not supposed to run, and you *know* it!"
10. "Please try to get your job done," instead of "Stop fooling around!"

Everyone is guilty of saying things the wrong way at times. We quote these sentences simply to emphasize the point that there *are* skilled ways of expressing ideas to boys and girls that take thought and reveal a general attitude.

Learn to say what you mean in the most courteous and effective manner possible.

3. *Ask questions carefully*. During conversations ask few questions which can be answered by "Yes" or "No." Any old guess has a fifty per cent chance of being right when such questions are asked. Even kindergarteners needn't be sloppy thinkers, and religion, of *all* things, demands our hearts, souls, and *minds*.

When you wish to keep the attention of the entire group, ask the question, then use the child's name. "Please bring the picture, Debbie," not "Debbie, please bring the picture."

Do not immediately utter right or wrong pronouncements on children's answers. Instead you may sometimes ask, "Do you agree with Billy, Sandy?" or "Is Billy right?" or "What do you think about it, Jo?" Of course it would be boring to always handle an answer in this way. Vary your response to include these and such replies as, "Good for you for remembering," or "Perhaps you had better think about that a little longer, Dot." What we want to avoid is the standard replies, "You're right," or "That's wrong." It is the teacher's job to help children think!

4. *Get the attention of the group quickly and effectively when you need it.* There are many occasions when the children are busy with various activities and the teacher needs to give some direction or convey some information. At these times use the same signal always so that children will come to know what it means and respond to it. This signal may be: (1) tapping a triangle slowly three times; (2) a series of four to six notes on the piano; or (3) a vocal direction, referred to as a directional songlet. These are not the only three possibilities; you may also "sing-talk" your directions, making up a simple tune to your direction. Any of these will work. When you have given the signal, stand still yourself and watch the children, mentioning the name of anyone who does not stand still and listen, "We are waiting for Gerry to be listening. Dave and Henry are ready." Do not try to give directions until you have the attention of the whole group. If you wait for it and work for it, children will soon learn to respond quickly.

When the children are already seated in a group and you want attention, the situation is different. This time an action poem, song, counting device, or occasionally the statement, "I have something to tell you when you are all ready," will bring a response. You will discover other devices as you watch experienced teachers and as you gain experience yourself.

Sometimes one child will go on talking to the child next to him because he is unaware that his attention is needed, or because he just prefers to go on talking anyway. Do not lose the attention of your group by directing remarks to him alone. Instead of becoming personal, as "Alan, please stop talking and listen," say "We would like to have Alan listen too. He is part of our group," or some similar approach. "We do not like to sit and wait for one child when there are so many things to do that are fun."

To get the attention of one child to whom you have something to say (while many activities are in progress in the room, for example), go to him, stoop down to his level and talk directly to him. Clapping your hands or calling across the room are relatively useless, add to the confusion of a room, and are not particularly courteous. You will save time and save interrupting everyone by using better methods of gaining attention.

It is amazing how much difference it makes in the atmosphere of a room and in your ability to accomplish a teaching job when you master the simple techniques of obtaining a good group response.

5. *Expect quiet only when necessary.* Kindergarteners are not naturally quiet. As a matter of fact, neither are grown-ups — witness the hubbub when twenty people are chatting over cakes and tea or exchanging remarks before the chairman calls the meeting to order! Some beginning teachers feel it is a tribute to their ability if they are able to keep the group quiet, so they are constantly hushing them, shushing them, and insisting on walking on tiptoes, all of which are highly unsuitable requirements. If the department is situated so that normal, happy kindergarten noise is going to disturb some other group in the Sunday church school, your board of Christian education needs to do something about it immediately. If you are in such a situation, you will need to substitute quieter activities for those suggested in your curriculum which are accompanied by considerable noise. Occasionally you also may want to give a listening signal and remind your group to be more quiet so that other children in a nearby area may hear their story.

Often when the group gets noisy there will be one child at the center of it, and the situation can be remedied by speaking to the one child individually or redirecting him into an activity which will demand more of his energy.

6. *Be aware of the physical situation.* The need for an adjustment in light, heat, or humidity will cause a group to get restless or listless. Anything less than ideal conditions will reduce the readiness of children to learn. Therefore the leading teacher has as an ongoing responsibility, the control of the facilities which determine light, temperature, and ventilation. The thermometer in your room should be placed at the

height of the chairs. Then remember that the floor is a little cooler. The temperature up around your shoulders and head when you are standing differs from that which the children are experiencing; therefore you will need to check the thermometer to make sure that your room is "not too warm and not too cold, but just right."

See that the conditions are adjusted whenever you note the room does not meet the ideal. The sky becomes overcast so the shades are opened or the lights turned on to continue to provide sufficient light in the room. The sun bursts forth brilliantly or creeps slowly around to shine directly on one of the work tables; the shade is closed to remedy this since children should not work with direct sunlight on their books or papers. If the room becomes hot and stuffy, turn off your radiator or open the windows, being careful children are not in a direct draft. Occasionally you may need to open your door for a quick change in ventilation; for this, choose a time when children are conversing or when the noise in the room will not disturb other groups.

Be sure when you are showing a book, picture, or object to the group that the light is good on what you want them to see. This means the light cannot be behind you, and you can never stand or sit in front of a window if you want children to see your face or what you are showing them.

If you have a rug, be sure it is not a "scratchy" one. If you have a very tall child, do not expect him to work at a low table or sit on a chair ten inches high. If a child is left-handed, do not squeeze him into a small work space next to a right-handed child. Do not have chairs or tables so grouped that some children need to climb over others to get in and out. Check your furniture occasionally, for tables will have a way of working over toward the cubbies, for example, so that the space for walking between is inadequate. Watch for safety hazards, such as a block on the floor in an unexpected place, or the corner of a table sticking out when the group is skipping.

All the physical aspects of the room as it meets the children's needs is the responsibility of the leading teacher or superintendent. Keep it as ideal as possible.

7. *Take a cue from the attention you are getting*. The at-

tention of the children is sometimes a measure for the success of the job you are doing. If they are not listening, it is not necessarily because they are badly trained or because they are contrary; it may mean that the teacher is not "on the ball" at that moment. So don't blame the children, but rather, analyze what the trouble is immediately and remedy it. Perhaps you have kept them sitting too long; maybe you are using the wrong tone, or the wrong material; or maybe they cannot hear you or see you well. It may be that you began the activity before you had the attention of everyone. Perhaps you are fighting against more attractive odds; Henry has a cricket in his pocket; the adults are singing lustily next door; or Kerry is sitting next to Johnny and those two never can become interested in anything when they are seated next to one another.

Sometimes when you note poor attention on the part of several children, it is better to abandon your plans momentarily and get "with the group." They are not with you, so you go to them and then you can take them along to where you want to go. But you cannot lead them when they are way off in one place and you are plowing bravely ahead in another! Therefore acknowledge the situation and make a different approach. "Let's put the storybook over here and finish it later on when we are all ready to listen. There was a church in the story; right now let's play we are families going to church. What song could we sing about going to church while we walk softly around the room?" Then come back to the story later, beginning at the beginning again.

Or you might say, "I see some of us feel like swinging our arms. Let's all stand up and swing our arms and we will have some clock music so your arms can be pendulums going back and forth and back and forth."

Then there is the funny thing that sometimes happens which wasn't in your plans for the session at all. There is no use ignoring it. Have a good laugh about it and then go back to what you were doing as a group saying, "That was very funny, but now it's time to get back to work. Alan is just half through with a very good picture over here and Jill and Peter need to work a little longer on their block building." Fellowship in laughter draws a group closer together.

But be sure you are never laughing at the expense of someone in the group. No one enjoys being laughed at. You can help the children develop maturity in this respect by your own response.

Interruptions and poor attention should be turned into immediate assets. Never battle against them blindly, for in such a battle, it seems as though the teacher always loses!

8. *Give children responsibilities for helping one another.* The kindergarten teacher is always feeling it might be nice to have a double pair of hands, for sometimes she could be helping two people at once. Occasionally she wishes she could be in two places at once! Adding staff members reduces the frequency of such occasions, but unfortunately there are times when teachers are absent for a last-minute reason or we have trouble finding a replacement for someone who has moved away, and we just find ourselves shorthanded.

In such a situation, children will usually respond by doing more than we expect. We are often surprised at the way they rise to the occasion. Children *need* to have the satisfaction of trying to do things for themselves and to have the fun of doing things for others as well. This is a fact which should be in our minds always and which should influence our procedures in the kindergarten.

After a short time with a group you begin to know which children are particularly capable in one way, which in another. Carol enjoys cleaning up and always does a thorough job, Ridge is excellent in working puzzles, Walter is always noticing what other children need, Eric can define any word that the group runs into. Here are resources within your group to be utilized. You will not therefore turn the cleaning jobs over to Carol and let Barry shirk his job one hundred per cent, nor yet ask Ridge to go to the immediate assistance of any child who has difficulty with a puzzle. It will still be important for every child to face up to his own responsibilities, and have the satisfaction of meeting them successfully. It will be of equal importance to avoid pointing out that one child can do easily what others have trouble doing.

The skillful teacher will be able to put to work in the room the special abilities of all the members of the group. She will encourage each child to do his very best, and will also call on his friends to work with him on a job that turns out to be a big one for him. So Ridge can be called on to help Sally with her puzzle before she gets completely discouraged; not to do it for her, remember, but to help her. Aware of these abilities, the teacher will need to guard against calling on one particular child frequently for assistance or making a feature of doing so. Children can help one another button smocks. They can help a child who has spilled a pan of pegs. They can share in a big putting-away-blocks job. An alert teacher can allocate to different children many of the things she might just go ahead and do herself if she didn't stop to think. One phase of this procedure which needs underscoring is this — always remember to thank the child who performed the service. Sometimes you may also want to suggest: "I believe Ted appreciates the help you've given him getting his paste jar open, Hal. Ted, wouldn't you like to tell Hal 'Thank you'?"

9. *Give each child a recognized place in the group.* This point already has been touched upon in more than one spot and is mentioned here only to make sure you do not overlook it. This effort on the part of the teacher to help each child know he has something worth while to contribute, to be aware that she believes in him, and to gain some appreciation from the group has a definite bearing on the spirit of a group. At the same time, it improves the response of the group as a whole because of the value they place upon one another. It also gives real practice in Christian living in a group. She does not permit the group to label a child, "Jan is bad. He runs away from home," but replies, "No, Jan is not bad. Sometimes Jan does things which are wrong. So does everybody. But Jan is trying to do the right things. We all have to try to do the right things, don't we?" Beware of the "scribes and the Pharisees"; they are to be found, in embryo, even in the kindergarten!

10. *Give the children all of your time.* There will be a temptation for the adults in the room to lapse into a discussion of irrelevant matters at times when everything seems to be under control. Whenever you feel tempted to talk about any subject not related to kindergarten, pinch yourself! Then

take a good look at the children. Somewhere you are needed! You are in the Sunday church school for *one* reason — to guide the children's Christian growth; the socializing can wait. Teachers will of course have things to say to one another during the session; indeed their friendliness toward one another is a matter to which the children are keenly sensitive. But the matters for conversation should be limited to talking about the children, the room, the program, the materials, and that conversation should be exchanged only which is necessary to the best interests of the group. Avoid discussing within earshot any matters not for children's ears. It is a mistake to let one child hear you say, "Timmy never finishes anything he starts. Have you noticed? Look, there's a picture half finished and now he has started a puzzle." Remember, "little pitchers have big ears" — bigger than ever these days and with a brain capacity to match!

11. *Utilize the children's ideas.* This too we have discussed before. Just for the sake of emphasis, it must be included here. It is very exciting to have a child come up with an idea that is really better than the one you had in mind. Include the children in planning projects. Get their ideas and opinions and permit them to work out the ones that are feasible. And if they come up with something you *had* thought of first, just keep it a secret and say, "I think that's an excellent idea, Rusty. We can certainly work that out!"

12. *Know how to make transitions from one activity to another.* Of major importance in the kindergarten morning is the leading teacher's manner of guiding the children from one activity to the next. If thought is not given to this matter, a great deal of valuable time will be wasted trying to get children to leave small interest groups and gather for Together Time. Again, when children are in a large group and it is time for individual work in creative activities, it can become frustrating for everyone unless the leading teacher has thought through the way this transition is to be accomplished. From lunch to rest, from rest to story, from story to game, and so on throughout the morning, time and again the need arises for making transitions to change the activity, location, and organization of the children. These transitions can be fun, but for the new teacher or for a teacher who does

not recognize that special thought and skill are required right at these points, they can be a source of difficulty. Such a teacher will frequently say, "Children, now we are all going to come over and sing." This sounds short enough and simple enough but the results of such an announcement can be a stampede. Four-to-six-year-olds *do* tend to stampede! It may be their eagerness to co-operate, it may be their desire for a new activity, it may be their boundless energy, but, whatever the reason, teachers who are careless in group directions at a transition time are asking for trouble.

It would be easier just to demonstrate how easily transitions can be made than it is to set down a series of principles. However, the following suggestions will be helpful to you:

(a) Get the attention of the group you wish to move.

(b) Give clearcut directions, telling who is to act and exactly what they are to do. Examples: "Ann's table may push in their chairs and get their resting mats"; "All the children with brown shoes may stand up. All the children with brown shoes may find places for juicetime"; "Mrs. Hill's family may get their workbooks"; "As soon as you have put away all your work materials, you may bring a chair over near the piano"; "When Clark touches your shoulder, you may get crayons and begin work."

(c) Move first any group that may block the traffic area.

(d) If your group is large, do not call everyone to act simultaneously; this might sound slower, but it will save time in the long run. Commend each group which follows directions well.

(e) Have something for children to look forward to. When they get where they are going, provide something more than sitting and waiting. Have a teacher there, ready to act as soon as a few children are ready.

(f) If children are moving chairs and you want them in a special formation, be there as they are arriving to help each child to place his chair in a satisfactory location. There are not many occasions for placing chairs formally, but you may be showing a filmstrip and want the chairs grouped in rows, or you may have a guest and want the chairs arranged so that each child can easily see the guest or get up to give him something.

(g) Visualize each transition before you give directions to the children. Try to follow a pattern for several Sundays using the same directions for the same transitions; then children will be able to follow very readily.

13. *Keep individual growth in mind and vary expectations and guidance of individuals to suit their individual needs.* Children who have never handled scissors before should not be expected to cut out a shape on a line. Children vary greatly in this respect. Expect each child to do his best. Express appreciation when he has done his best, even though the results may not measure up to the work of another child. God has made each of us different and that makes our world an interesting place in which to live. It is the teacher's responsibility to see that each child is offered a challenge at his level of development, is called upon to reach and grow a little, but not to stretch too much all at once. Suit assigned tasks to the child, therefore, and see that he gains the satisfaction of accomplishing them successfully.

14. *Stop undesirable behavior at once.* This suggestion refers to the type of behavior which is often contagious. A little experience will show you that when children do socially unacceptable things, with one eye on the teacher to see whether she will do anything about it, you "better had" do something. Children are reaching for limits in such cases and really want you to redirect them. If this is the situation, they will try something else and something else, until you *have* to recognize their behavior. You might as well recognize it in the beginning, ask the child to come to you and give him something special to do or let him know that this is not the kind of behavior we expect in kindergarten. Just because this is a Sunday church school does not mean that you are under the necessity of permitting *any* type of behavior. The children may look adorable in their nylon ruffles and long trousers and bow ties, but there is no magic which transforms them into angels when they walk through the church door; so don't expect it!

15. *Set a standard of response.* Children will soon learn what you expect if you are consistent about expecting it, and they will be eager to please the teacher. One way of making this standard known, and of inspiring others to measure up

to it, is to offer encouragement and praise to children who put forth an effort and achieve. There is no incentive so strong as the incentive to earn the commendation of the teacher, it seems. A child who is kindly complimented on the way he is carrying his chair or cleaning up, or working on a picture, or sharing his crayons will redouble his efforts in the warm glow. There is no need in the kindergarten to "call the group down." If they get "out of hand," it is usually the teacher's failure, not the children's; so scolding does nothing to raise a behavior standard, but praise will do amazing things!

16. *Know what is going on everywhere all the time.* Now this is a hard one! There is, however, no way of escaping the necessity of this requirement. Because it is basic, we have reserved it for our last point for emphasis. A kindergarten leading teacher must have the capacity, while she is helping a child in the storybook corner, of knowing what is going on in the rest of the room without making the child she is helping feel that her mind is only partly with him. She cannot help one child so exclusively that she is totally unaware of what is happening elsewhere. It is helpful, when dealing with one child or group, to stand with one's back to a wall and thus have a view of the room. Knowing what children may do characteristically, she will provide ahead of time for every situation possible, then she will keep abreast of the children's activities and their needs. It is most helpful to have teachers assigned to various areas of responsibility when there are several teachers in a room, for this greatly simplifies the requirements for each one. The leading teacher should circulate from one to another during the times when they are working individually or in small groups, making many short contacts rather than any extended ones.

These specific suggestions for obtaining a good group response have come from watching many teachers at work. The methods of working have been effective for other teachers, and as you make them (or adaptations of them) your own, they will work for you also. Yes, teaching a group, however small the group, is different from teaching just one child, but your rewards will be multiplied as you grow in the skills required for calling forth a good group response.

> Father, we thank thee for thy wisdom in placing children in families to learn, and in planning for the satisfactions of human living to come not from isolated living, but from community living. Help us as teachers to put into practice the Christian principles of kindness and consideration, and to know how to develop these in the boys and girls we teach. Grant us wisdom in understanding how a group can live and work together best, and help us to develop the skills needed for guiding boys and girls as they work and play, worship and learn together. This we pray because we are full of eagerness to show them the way to live constantly with and for thee. Amen.

## Projects and Discussion Questions

1. Observe a skilled teacher and discuss how she puts into practice the principles explained in this chapter.
2. Make a study of vocabulary suitable for the kindergarten. List thirty words a teacher might be tempted to use with kindergarten children which might be beyond their understanding.
3. Discuss ways in which a teacher may help children in the group to find a recognized place.
4. What are several types of undesirable behavior which call for action on the teacher's part? Suggest possible action suited to each.
5. What standards of response should be set up in the teacher's mind? What safety habits are important? What basic patterns of individual consideration for other members of the group? How important is consistency on the teacher's part in expecting children to measure up to the standards? How can the teacher convey a set of standards to the group without being either stuffy or domineering?

CHAPTER 6

## WORKING ON A TEAM

The early church set a pattern of togetherness, not "I" and "you" but "we," and the church of today has no place for single-handed ventures either. We are all members one of another, differing in gifts, in responsibilities, but as indispensable to one another as the eye is to the hand, and the ear to the foot. This pattern of togetherness pertains to the kindergarten as vitally as it does to other areas of the church.

Each personality has something distinct to contribute; some function which cannot be performed by any of the others, or by all of them put together. There is a place for creativity and ingenuity in the Kindergarten Department, and nothing would be duller than to have everyone carry on his work in exactly the same way.

There is a common ground in our purposes and the basic qualities required of every kindergarten teacher are the same. Probably no one fully measures up to the qualifications offered here, but as in the case of the ideal kindergarten room toward which we work, so we need to have in mind the type of person we would like to be and will try to become if we are to do the best job possible. Though we may vary in the extent to which we meet each of these qualifications, if we are eager to grow toward the ideal, and will work to do so, we can meet the basic requirements for the job.

Leaders in the church are sometimes guilty of "playing down" the qualifications of teachers. Examine yourself carefully and honestly. Are you qualified, or willing to become qualified, to teach?

## QUALIFICATIONS OF TEACHERS

Use the check-chart below as a basis for checking your qualifications.[1]

_____ 1. A dynamic Christian faith.
_____ 2. A sincere love for and growing appreciation for the kindergarten child.
_____ 3. A friendly, outgoing approach to other people.
_____ 4. A genuine smile and a sense of humor.
_____ 5. A pleasing, expressive, well-modulated voice.
_____ 6. A relaxed attitude, freedom from tension. (A jerky, abrupt person is no candidate!)
_____ 7. A keen sense of responsibility.
_____ 8. The capacity to develop patience and understanding.
_____ 9. The capacity to work as a member of a team, with a congenial give and take, and willingness to take suggestions.
_____ 10. A neat and attractive appearance.
_____ 11. The ability to approach a problem with ingenuity, resourcefulness, creativeness and determination.
_____ 12. Sincerity in dealing with people.
_____ 13. Alertness and concern for doing a job well.
_____ 14. Willingness to learn; eagerness to grow.
_____ 15. A concern for the church and for its whole program.

While this list may seem to present a somewhat discouraging (because so idealistic) picture, it is reassuring to note that a great many people possess all these characteristics in some measure. It is further true that almost any quality on this list can be developed when an individual is aware of the need for it.

### What has the church a right to expect of a teacher?

Accepting a responsibility in the church school is not an act which should be performed as a favor to anyone nor should it be an acquiescence to the coaxing and pleading of leaders who have a vacancy with no one to fill it. It should be accepted as a privilege and in a spirit of consecration to God who is calling us to such service. It should be accepted

[1] Adapted from *Kindergarten Superintendent's Book*, by Lois Horton Young. Philadelphia, The Judson Press, 1956. Used by permission.

with both a prayer and a sense of obligation and, this being the case, church leaders have a right to expect a new teacher to have: (1) a willingness to work; (2) a willingness to learn, yea, a *determination* to keep growing so that a better and better job can be done, and (3) a clearcut purpose. The church can also expect the teacher to accept every child for what he is; to love him and take him into the group, although he may have "unacceptable" physical, behavioral, social or economic characteristics. We say again and yet again, that no teacher ever "arrives," for teaching is an adventure in growing, and requires the realization that there is no limit to the growth that can be ours as we adventure with God and with children along this road.

## GROWING SPIRITUALLY

There is no such thing as remaining static spiritually. We either grow or we shrink. Our lives are either fed by the eternal springs of daily and hourly fellowship with God or they dry up and become barren and unproductive.

We cannot give spiritual guidance to others unless our resources are constantly being renewed, and to this end we must seek God in prayer, in worship, and in reading the Bible. Prayer will give us power, worship will give us insight, reading the Bible will give us wisdom.

Spiritual growing is a part of all of life. It is not just praying more, though it is more constant awareness of God, more ready communication with him. It is not just attending more meetings and services at the church although few people grow spiritually if they are irregular in church attendance. It is not just reading the Bible regularly, though there is no spiritual growth without exposing oneself daily to God's direction and letting his Word speak to us. Spiritual growth is much more. It is a daily growth toward more Christlike living, facing life's problems with a more fully Christian viewpoint, having the mind of Christ in our relationships with other people, growing in our capacity to apply Christian truth to every area of our lives. To be growing in these ways is the obligation of every teacher.

It is difficult to measure spiritual growth and yet, somehow, one "knows" when a person is walking close to God.

## RELATIONSHIPS AMONG TEACHERS

The attitude of the teachers within a room toward one another has a significant effect upon the spirit of the room and a direct effect upon the children's concept of the Christian fellowship. They are highly sensitive to the atmosphere created by the feelings of individuals for one another. Attempts to hide sensitivities, fears and animosities from children are futile.

For this reason it is essential for the members of the kindergarten staff to have a genuine feeling of regard for one another, and to have the conviction that working together is *fun!* Nobody can afford to feel that his way is the only way to do a job. Nobody can afford to feel that a suggestion about the way he does something is a personal criticism. Nobody can afford to feel that another staff member does not like him. When teachers feel any of these things, the work of the kindergarten suffers. That is how closely knit the staff is; that is how much of a team it really is.

Relationships between staff members can be improved by the habit of expressing appreciation to one another. If a member does something helpful for another member, or does a particularly good job of some phase of the work, an expression of appreciation not only can have an encouraging effect upon her, but also can build up ties between teachers. Never allow a misunderstanding to develop; it will flourish if kept in the dark, but if brought to light and discussed frankly between the people involved, it will evaporate. Send birthday cards to one another. Go out to lunch together once in a while, or, if the entire staff is not free during the day, get together to do something in the evening occasionally just to enjoy one another's fellowship and to get better acquainted. In a kindergarten where you have a large staff, it will be a rich experience to put into a basket once a month folded papers on each of which is written the name of a staff member. Then each person, drawing one out, prays daily for the one whose name she finds. Praying for a person really brings them close to you and releases God's power for them in a marvelous way. As you study the situation, other ways will occur to you for bringing staff members closer together.

## WORKING TOGETHER AS A TEAM

Signals are called and the ball is in play. Every man knows his job and does it. He has a place to be and he is there! At times one job may be more spectacular than another, but no one job is more important than another. Every member of the team is necessary.

The work of the kindergarten calls for a sharing of ideas and responsibilities that can be adequately done only when the group sits down together and plans. The "let not your right hand know what your left hand doeth" policy was never meant to apply to a team of church school teachers and can end only in confusion. At the beginning of the year, the staff will need to map out plans and responsibilities and to look ahead to see what units will be included in the course of the next twelve months. There may be a brainstorming session to get down ideas everyone can contribute to any phase of program, equipment, parent-relations; then these may be laid aside for consideration and classification. Next give all teachers their copies of the enrollment. Now go to work on the first unit, laying out what is to be done and which is the area of responsibility for each person. (See pages 48-49 for discussion of unit planning.)

Thereafter before each new unit is begun, meet to lay plans for the new unit. This will make your get-togethers almost monthly in frequency. These meetings also should include some discussion in other areas — equipment, relations with parents, and so forth. Include also a time of spiritual inspiration and refreshment and you will have a meeting to which your staff will look forward. If possible set a regular time for these planning meetings to save having to struggle to set a date at each meeting. Plan also to go as a group to institutes, workshops, and demonstrations in the area of your work.

The allocation of responsibility is the job of the kindergarten superintendent, but jobs will be assigned and accepted in team-planning sessions mentioned above. In a one-room kindergarten, the superintendent is also the leading teacher and is responsible for the entire program, usually conducting those parts where all the children are together. Helping teachers will be assigned to small groups.

In a church with a kindergarten attendance of more than 20 children, it is strongly recommended that the group be divided on an age basis with a leading teacher responsible for each group. The superintendent of the total kindergarten may be one of these leading teachers. Each group would have its helping teachers (one for every five or six children).

The leading teacher need not be the same person throughout the year. If you have more than one teacher, each equally capable of guiding the entire group for the specific times mentioned, the responsibility for serving in this way may be assigned to one teacher for the duration of a unit, then during the next unit another teacher may serve as leading teacher.

The arrangement of teachers and their responsibilities is a fluid rather than a static thing, but whatever arrangement is followed, the staff is still a team, working together for the spiritual growth of the kindergarten children.

## PARENTS AND TEACHERS TOGETHER

Not only does a team spirit need to pervade the relationships of teachers within the kindergarten, but such a spirit needs to exist between teachers and parents of children in the church school also. The teachers need to be aware that the efforts of the church school need to be related to the efforts of the home, and that the church school's role is one of supplementing the home. How can parents and teachers work together so that they too form a team, co-operating to bring about Christian growth in the children with whom all are so vitally concerned?

### Parents' Materials

This material is usually included in the curriculum materials and needs to be sent into the home in a manner that calls attention to its value. It may be delivered to the home by a personal call, mailed or handed to the parents as they call for their children at the kindergarten room. Perhaps rather than using one method of distribution throughout the year, you may wish to vary the method from one quarter to the next. For the first time, at least, it would be more helpful to the parent to have the teacher visit in the home and interpret the use of his piece of material.

### A Parents' Bulletin Board

Just outside your room would be an ideal place to put a bulletin board, "For Parents Only." Here you can call attention to special activities of the kindergarten. You can cut up and mount excerpts from the current parents' material, put up pieces of work by the children, announcements, and sometimes pictures or clippings of interest. Make the bulletin board colorful and eye-catching, and change it often. Different staff members may be assigned the responsibility for the board or a person who has a flair for advertising or displays may be asked to carry this on-going project, receiving materials from all kindergarten staff members for use. If there is no space outside the room, it may be placed in the room near the door, on a portable screen in the hall, or even on the door itself.

### Visits to the Department

After the children have adjusted to the kindergarten group, visits to the kindergarten room may be arranged for different parents on different Sundays. Most parents are very much interested in knowing what goes on in the kindergarten and many of them will be happy to know that they are wanted. Provision should be made for their comfortable seating in inconspicuous places. Having only one couple at a time will prevent the undesirable situation of having them converse. However, if space permits, two or three couples may be invited on a given Sunday. They could be spaced around the room to eliminate conversation. Children like to introduce Mother and Daddy. Parents should be prepared for the possibility that their children will not participate in the same manner as they do when their own parents are not present.

Children will become accustomed to having extra adults sitting in the room and will take them very much as a matter of course after a few Sundays.

### Calls in the Home

One of the things teachers often have trouble finding time to do is calling in the homes of their children. And yet, it is a tremendous event in the life of the child when his teacher comes to visit. Usually you will find the call is much appreciated by the parent also. A third value is the larger understanding of the child which can be gained from seeing him in his home environment and in circumstances outside the church kindergarten group. Finally, the teacher finds it a most rewarding and strengthening experience. Such a call should be purposeful, its objective being to show the parents that the church is really interested in their family and stands ready to be helpful to them in any way possible in their responsibility for the Christian training of their child. This call might come in connection with the distribution of the parents' material for the new quarter or the teacher might take along some other appealing piece of literature—a leaflet on teaching the child to pray, or on good books for young children, or on the child's concept of God, for example.

In all our contacts with parents we want to make it clear that the church is eager to be helpful to the parents, not that parents are responsible for helping the church to carry out some program or project with the children. We need to bring parents to the realization that we feel the need for working *with* them, and for having their help in planning with the church for their children's spiritual growth.

On any visit to the home the child will probably be eager to show his treasures and will think of the teacher as *his* guest as well as a visitor to his parents. The teacher will show by her friendliness and responsiveness to the child that this is her point of view too.

## Meetings of Parents and Teachers

Parents are busy people but like the rest of us they usually find time for the things they most want to do. Therefore, when we set up a meeting of parents and teachers, the secret of getting a good response will be in making them *want* to come. Include these elements in the meeting and you will have something to interest every individual, providing each part of the program is well planned and interestingly done: a period of fellowship and getting acquainted (this might start the meeting off occasionally rather than coming at the end; food and name tags and background music on a record player melt the ice fast!); a learning feature in the form of a film, a speaker, a demonstration, or a panel, making each meeting completely different; an opportunity to talk about their children (every parent's favorite subject); a time for inspiration (a short and stirring devotional presentation).

Make the atmosphere an informal one. It is amazing how much difference attention to a few details will make. An attractive flower arrangement, chairs arranged informally, a hostess to greet each arriving couple, a pair of lighted hurricane lamps on the piano—these touches which speak of warm concern and friendliness have a real effect on people as soon as they come in, and contribute to their enthusiasm about the meeting and about coming back the next time. Be creative about planning the meetings and about introducing variety and surprise into the meeting place and the program. The more effort you put in, the better results you get out. It will be better to have one top-notch meeting a year than to have four mediocre ones!

This will be a good time to have open house in your room. The children will enjoy having a share in getting the room ready at the session before the meeting if you talk with them about the fact that the "mommies and daddies" are coming to visit. Kindergarten parents' meetings may be held separately from the total church school and be very effective.

## Department Parents

As a means to closer parent-teacher relations, you may want to invite some parents to serve in a special capacity. Select one couple for about every eight or ten children in your group to serve as department parents. This group of parents can help in planning parents' meetings, in forming a telephone squad to get information around to other parents, in assisting in special projects, in helping to secure equipment. To increase friendliness between parents, you will find it a valuable aid to duplicate enrollment lists and see that every parent of a child in the department has a copy. On this list will be the name, address, telephone, birthday, and parents' first names of all the children in the kindergarten.

Parents are a wonderful resource for the kindergarten teacher who learns how to utilize them. When they feel they have a part, their interest is multiplied a hundredfold. When they are informed about what is going on, they usually are more than glad to help in any way they can. Some kindergartens send home a quarterly newsletter to fill this need.

## OTHER RESOURCES IN YOUR COMMUNITY

What other places in the community are important to the children in your group? Where else do they spend their time besides at home and at church? Make a list of these and then make a point of becoming familiar with them.

Plan to visit the public kindergarten or private nursery school. Not only will you see your pupils in their weekday environment but also you will receive new ideas to use in church school. If you do not take too much time, the teacher will probably answer questions after the children leave. Write a note of appreciation later.

Visit the library where your children go, and make a friend of the librarian; she will be happy to help you with resource books for your own enrichment and with books to use on your kindergarten book table to accompany certain units. Think of this library as a place where your children go and let them know that you go there too. Refer to the librarian by name as a friend.

Visit the stores where your children go, the local zoo, and nearby points of interest to which they go. These visits will give you a better background for teaching and a common bond with the children. Make the things that are important to them important to you.

## WORKING WITH YOUR PASTOR

The work of the kindergarten should tie in with the work of the church as a whole. It is your responsibility to support the work of your church in every way possible both as an individual and as a teacher of boys and girls. You will be able to give your children a sense of fellowship with the church as a whole in innumerable ways if you remain alert to opportunities for doing this. Share with them the satisfactions of church improvements. Let them know what is going on in the church program which might be of interest to them. For instance, in regard to improvement, perhaps the lawn has been seeded, a new piano has been purchased for the Junior Department, or some of the daddies have just painted the foyer a lovely shade of green. In regard to the program, perhaps the children's choir is going to sing at the community Christmas tree lighting. (This will mean some of their big brothers and sisters and friends.) Someday they may be a part of the children's choir. Give the kindergarteners opportunities to share in any appropriate church projects, making cards for a grandmother who has broken her leg, bringing white gifts for a children's home, or contributing to a clothing collection for Church World Service.

Introduce to the children older friends who might come into the room. There will be planned occasions, of course, for visits from church friends, but we will never want to overlook the learning situations that come unexpectedly.

We should seek especially to build up a relationship between the children and the pastor, for he should be the friend of every one of them. See that he has written memoranda of cases of accident or serious illness, changes of address, new babies, and visitors of which you become aware. Let him know that you are eager to work with him in any way he can suggest. Pray for him personally and pray for him occasionally in the kindergarten class.

There is a thrill in being part of a team which accomplishes a task together. Teaching in the kindergarten is an experience of sharing with others to achieve results — others on the staff, in the church, in the community, and parents in the home. One plants, another waters, another offers tender loving care, and God gives the increase — the growth of boys and girls into maturing Christians, who love and serve him.

The kind of Christian the child becomes, or whether he becomes one at all, may depend on the way you, the kindergarten teacher, interpret the Bible and the Christian way of life to him. Your responsibility is great, but you will find that working with God in carrying out that responsibility leads *you* into a closer walk with him. This is the joy that lies before you in the adventure of teaching kindergarten children!

> Father, we thank thee for the thrilling adventure of teaching little children. We know ourselves to be unworthy of this privilege, and inadequate to accomplish the high goals we set. Give us the openness of eye and heart to discover all the ways we can work with others and involve them in this exciting experience. Give us the tact to know how to present to them winsomely specific tasks which may contribute to the spiritual growth of the boys and girls in the kindergarten. Help us to work as though every effort of ours is essential and to pray as though all depends on thee. In his name, who has opened for us the door into abundant living and joyous service, Christ our Lord, Amen.

## Projects and Discussion Questions

1. Rate yourself honestly, using the chart on page 100.
2. Prepare a list of ten briefly stated questions (based on pages 100 to 109) which you believe will be helpful to you in doing a good teaching job.
3. What pattern is followed by your church kindergarten staff for
   (a) Interstaff fellowship,
   (b) Planning together,
   (c) Working with parents.
   Discuss ways you think one of these might be enriched.
4. How would you go about establishing a group of "class parents"? What specific services might they perform in your church kindergarten?
5. If there is a kindergarten or preschool in your community which is attended by children from your church, arrange to visit and observe there.
6. Visit your local library and examine the collection of books for young children. Select three which might have value in the church kindergarten. Show and discuss these in your leadership education class.

# BIBLIOGRAPHY OF HELPFUL MATERIALS

## BOOKS

Allstrom, Elizabeth, *Let's Play A Story,* Friendship Press, N. Y.

Brown, Jeanette Perkins, *The Storyteller in Religious Education,* Pilgrim Press, Boston, Mass.

Fritz, Dorothy B., *The Spiritual Growth of Children,* Westminster Press, Philadelphia, Pa.

Gesell, Arnold, *The First Five Years of Life,* Harper and Brothers, N. Y.

Hymes, James L., Jr., *A Child Development Point of View,* Prentice-Hall, Englewood-Cliffs, N. J.

Hymes, James L., Jr., *Behavior and Misbehavior,* Prentice-Hall, Englewood-Cliffs, N. J.

Keiser, Armilda B., *Here's How and When,* Friendship Press, N. Y.

Lobingier, Elizabeth Miller, *Activities in Child Education,* Pilgrim Press, Boston, Mass.

Miller, Madeleine S. and J. L., *Harper's Bible Dictionary,* Harper and Brothers, N. Y.

Sheehy, Emma D., *There's Music in Children,* Henry Holt & Co., N. Y.

Shields, Elizabeth McE. and Mallard, Dorothae G., *Guiding Kindergarten Children in the Church School,* John Knox Press, Richmond, Va.

Smither, Ethel, *The Use of the Bible with Children,* Abingdon Press, N. Y.

Strang, Ruth, *A Study of Young Children,* Abingdon Press, N. Y.

Welker, Edith F., *Friends with All the World,* Friendship Press, N. Y.

Whitehouse, Elizabeth, *The Children We Teach,* Judson Press, Philadelphia, Pa.

Wills, Clarice D. and Stegeman, Wm. H., *Living in the Kindergarten,* Follett Publishing Co., Chicago, Ill.

Young, Lois H., *Kindergarten Superintendent's Book,* Judson Press, Philadelphia, Pa.

## MAGAZINES

*Childhood Education,* 1200 Fifteenth St., N.W., Washington 5, D. C.
*International Journal of Religious Education,* Box 238, New York 10, N. Y.

## RECORDS

*Home and Church Songs* Album, Bethany Press, St. Louis, Mo.
*Kindergarten Songs and Rhythms* Album, Judson Press, Philadelphia, Pa.

## EQUIPMENT

Community Playthings, Rifton, N. Y.
Creative Playthings, 5 University Pl., N. Y. 3, N. Y.
Play-Art Educational Equipment, 437-439 Arch St., Philadelphia 6, Pa.